CONTEMPLATION

INTIMACY IN A DISTANT WORLD

Other books by David F. Allen, M.D.

Ethical Issues in Mental Retardation: Tragic Choices/Living Hope
The Cocaine Crisis
Crack: The Broken Promise
In Search of the Heart
Shattering the Gods Within

CONTEMPLATION
INTIMACY IN A DISTANT WORLD

David F. Allen, M.D.

Curtain Call Productions, LLC
McLean, Virginia

Art Director: Craig Maher
Graphic Designer: Paul Gaschler
Cover Photo: Michael Kleinberg
email: craigmaherdesign@verizon.net

ISBN: 0 - 9753306 - 0 - 8
1 3 5 7 9 10 8 6 4 2

Printed in the United States of America
Published by Curtain Call Productions, LLC.
Curtain Call Productions: 6809 Sorrel Street, McLean Virginia, 22101, USA
email: dougcoppi@curtaincallproductions.com
phone: 703.753.2202

This book is dedicated to my adult Sunday School class at the Fourth Presbyterian Church in Bethesda, Maryland. Thank you so very much for sharing with me the opportunity to explore a deeper spirituality.

CONTENTS

Part One: The Fundamentals

Part Two: Contemplation In The Lives Of God's People

PROLOGUE: THE PARABLE OF PUDGY

Pudgy was a little fish that lived on the western end of Nassau in the Bahamas. His parents warned him that he shouldn't swim too close to the shore because the large waves, especially around the month of October, would wash him up onto the beach and he would die.

But Pudgy knew best. As far as he was concerned he could swim better than his parents or siblings; after all he had gone to a better swimming school than all of them. So, against the advice of his elders, one October morning Pudgy went swimming close to the beaches on the western end of Nassau. A large wave tossed him up on the beach and, as he watched the water ebb away, he realized that he was beached. He flipped his tail. He twisted his body. He tried to jump off the sand, but try as he might; he was unable to get back into the beautiful aquamarine sea. Afraid and trapped, he now remembered all his parents had told him; after all, hindsight is twenty-twenty.

As the Bahamian sun grew hotter, water evaporated from Pudgy and he became weaker. As the morning wore on, Pudgy went into early shock. He tried and tried to get back into the water, but the waves lapped just short of him, leaving him stranded. His heart beat faster and his fear now turned to terror.

Along the beach came a very sophisticated lady. Fascinated by the spectacle of the little fish on the beach, she stooped down to tell him how excited she was to meet him. But even before she could open her mouth, Pudgy blurted out his plea for help, crying, "Please help me, I'm beached. Put me back into the water—a fish out of water will die."

"Oh," said the lady, "I understand, but you see I belong to the Bahamas Independent Society and we believe that if people are just given the chance to help themselves, they can handle their problems much more effectively. In fact, I am on my way to the Independent Society meeting at our church down the street. So, little fish, you just keep on trying and I'm sure you will be able to do it all by yourself."

"Please help me," cried Pudgy growing ever weaker.
"Please put me back into the sea, you can even kick me back into the sea. A fish...out......of water...........will.................DIE."

"Don't be preposterous," replied the lady. "I would never kick one of God's little creatures, in fact I volunteer at the animal society weekly; God knows I would never harm one of his vulnerable little animals, so don't think like that, just keep on trying. You know the saying, 'Try and try again, boys, and you will succeed at last.' Anyway, I must be off to my meeting now—but I'll stop by on my way back and we can discuss your position further. Cheerio, and have a good day."

Pudgy tried again and again but became progressively weaker until he could hardly move. He was almost dead. Then a little girl came walking along the beach. Seeing Pudgy she stopped and quickly scooped him back into the water. "Now that's better!" she said smiling as Pudgy slowly regained his strength and started his journey home.

A little later our lady returned to the beach to check on Pudgy. When she arrived at the spot where Pudgy had been, she exclaimed in a loud, joyous voice, "I knew he could do it, I will never forget that little fish. He is now swimming with all the other fishes in the Bahamian sea. He had a problem, and, just like we said in our meeting this morning, he faced it. Now he is swimming happily ever after with all the other little fishes in the sea." The little girl, who was playing in the sand nearby, spoke up.

"No, that's not what happened. He was dying so I rescued him; I put him back into the sea. If I hadn't, he would have died."

What was lacking between the woman and the fish? They spent time together; she stopped long enough to hear him explain his inner longing, his need for survival. She talked with him, she encouraged him, she advised him, she even sought to nurture and motivate him, and she tried to build up his strength and self-esteem. She then took the time to come back and check up on him; in our modern scientific lingo, she did a follow-up study. But she didn't meet Pudgy's need. This lady was not malevolent. In fact she rejoiced at the thought of the fish conquering his problems and swimming happily in the sea again. But she didn't meet Pudgy's need. Her formidable intellect and education did not help her to connect. Does this parable remind us of the lack of intimacy that exists in the modern world? Overwhelmed by the powerful information revolution and our exciting new technologies, we grope toward a global village—but deep in our hearts we feel a paralyzing distance from each other. We can be involved with each other, spend time with each other, but still so easily miss each other. Pudgy is that friend who calls out to us for help. Pudgy is our husband who is trying to tell us that things are not well and are falling apart. Pudgy is our wife who screams in silence, warning us that her heart is breaking. Most sadly, Pudgy is our child. Seeing our children daily, we continue to ignore the cry of their hearts and the pain of their existences. And one day the cry stops. No, the pain did not go away, it was buried and over time that part of the heart died. Pudgy is also our own heart, which calls us by day and night, asking us to stop, to slow down, to take some time to smell the roses, to give up destructive habits, or just to become authentic. But one day the heart is silent. No, its needs did not go away, but that part of the heart died. A person dies many times before they die. The tragedy of life is not death itself, but that we allow so much of ourselves to die before we die, some of us living 40 to 60 percent below our potential. The challenge is to keep our childhood simplicity without being childish.

In this story the woman's idea about independent self-determination is very good and reasonable, but it is not applicable to helping the fish in its desperate situation. In spite of the perceived closeness, there was an empathic block between the heart of the woman and the heart of the fish, making it difficult for the woman to hear the fish's cry for help. She was caught up in the prison of the familiar, addicted to her internal idea of independence, which she projected onto the fish instead of listening to its cry. Seeing only her internal representation, the ideas in her head, she was able to ignore the external reality around her. Sadly this is not uncommon in the way we live. Made in the image of God, we are born into intimacy with God but have to discover or come to an awareness of that reality. We cannot be without the presence of God, but it is possible to live without the awareness of his presence. Through contemplation we can discover intimacy with God—he calls us to a total transformation of consciousness so that our lives are based on his love. This is manifest by a new ability to see the world as God sees it, to care for each other, and by an empathic concern for the environment.

ACKNOWLEGEMENTS

A book of this nature involves so many persons who have blessed me with their writing and thinking that it would be impossible to thank them all. Many fellow travellers have graced my life by sharing their insights, their love, and their companionship. I am truly grateful to them all, and what I present is just a fraction of what they have taught me. I am indebted to Jane Whitten for her excellent editing of this manuscript; her deep commitment and tireless work have made the book possible. I particularly appreciate the many insights that she brought to clarify difficult concepts. Her willing attitude and hard work has been a special encouragement to me. I would also like to thank Dr. Eolene Boyde-Macmillan of Cambridge University whose insights and in-depth questioning compelled me to examine the subject of contemplation from an academic perspective. I also would like to thank my beloved wife Victoria who has been the backbone of my writing and thinking, pushing me to clarify concepts and to keep a Biblical perspective always in mind. I am grateful to Caru Jones and Anita Fountain who typed and retyped the manuscript. I would like to thank my dear friend Dr. Ross McKenzie of the Chautauqua Institution who encouraged me to pursue the pathway of contemplative prayer. I must also make special mention of Dr. Gerald May of the Shalem Institute of Bethesda, Maryland, who in the time he acted as my spiritual director, introduced me to the deeper spiritual perspective of contemplative thinking and prayer. Obviously there is much more to learn, but my prayer is that where I fail and fall short, others travelling along will be able to fill in the gaps and lead people to a deeper understanding of the power and love of God which is expressed in the grace which is ever present, though sometimes unseen.

INTRODUCTION

This book, *Contemplation: Intimacy in a Distant World*, is the third book in a trilogy. The first was *In Search of the Heart* and the second was *Shattering the Gods Within*.

In the first book, *In Search of the Heart*, I discuss the importance of living life from the center, the heart. The heart, like the center of a bicycle wheel, is where all the spokes or issues of our lives converge. Only as we live from that center are we able to touch and be touched by our deepest or true selves as well as the selves of others. In this book I describe that life is wounded and that in order to liberate ourselves we have to work through our hurt trails to be able to open to our love story. Committing to love simply means opening to the experience of God's presence in our lives and recognizing that the presence is manifested by his loving care, which spreads between us as well as throughout nature. I discuss seven attitudes of the heart that are important in developing our spiritual and psychological life: love, communion, facing the heart's resistance, humility, simplicity, service, and transcendence.

The second book, *Shattering the Gods Within*, describes how once we face our hearts we find much resistance to God, our deeper selves, and love in the world. The book discusses how six major pseudo-gods or addictions in modern culture block the heart: narcissism, conformity, materialism, the sacredness of the affect, the bane of the extraordinary, and the illusion of permanence. The book deals with the shattering of these pseudo-gods or addictions of modern culture as a way to open our hearts to the love that will not let us go, and the face that does not turn away.

In this present book, *Contemplation: Intimacy in a Distant World*, my goal is to go beyond the search for the heart and the shattering of our resistances to love, to encourage us to live from our hearts—by moving from our false selves to open to our true selves in God. I realize that my experience fails to live up to the concepts presented, but my encouragement is that in contemplation we can never say we have arrived. My humble attempt is to paint an outline, which hopefully will be filled out by others whose experiences transcend mine. My thesis is that even though, with our modern telecommunications revolution, we communicate more than ever these days, we say less and have become less intimate. Intimacy is only possible if we are willing to live through our hearts. As the microcosm of our lives, our hearts have psychological, cognitive, and spiritual dimensions. In Part One I discuss the relationship between contemplation, spirituality, and intimacy. I also consider soullessness, anger as a brutal gift, the origin and function of the false self, the dynamics of contemplative prayer, and the concept of the true self. In Part Two I revisit these themes in scripture: Abraham's call to faith, the role of contemplation and rejection in the life of David, Mary Magdalene and her deep commitment to our Lord, and loving despite a shattered dream in the lives of Ruth and Naomi. The epilogue illustrates that although the pain of life may destroy intimacy, we can still follow God in love to experience a deeper compassion, to create intimacy in a distant world. Is this not the meaning of life?

Part One: The Fundamentals

CHAPTER 1
SPIRITUALITY, CONTEMPLATION, AND INTIMACY

The world without is desolate...except for the world within. (Wallace Stevens[1])

A very complex phenomenon in our modern culture, intimacy has a paradoxical ring. A lady who had been married for thirty years explained that recently she found herself going through a roller coaster experience of different feelings. She said, "I love my husband and we have, throughout the years, worked hard together to raise our family and live a respectable life style. When he leaves on a trip, although I miss him very much, these days I am not excited about his return: sometimes when he comes home I feel lonely. I just don't understand these feelings. How could a person that I love and have spent so much time with make me feel lonely?" Frustrated, she sighed and said, "Maybe it's something inside of me."

On another occasion Mary, a well educated, sophisticated lady, consulted me saying that she wanted to improve her ability to be open and loving to people around her, especially her children, but because her husband had hurt her during their marriage, she was intensely angry with him. She warned me that if ever our work together started to decrease her anger towards her husband, she would fire me. For ten sessions we worked extremely closely together. Mary talked about her childhood, her abusive father, how she felt that she had worked through that pain, and how, through much struggle, she had raised her children to become successful and meaningful citizens. The fly in the ointment was that she had been hurt deeply by her husband and there was no way she could find it in her heart to forgive him. She did not want to leave him, but wanted to stay with him so that she could return some of the pain that he had caused her: she was extremely angry with him. When we approached the subject of her relationship with her husband, during our work together, she would remain quiet and say she did not want to talk about it. Periodically, during our ten sessions together, Mary would talk about the pain he had caused her and then a small tear would appear; but when she caught herself feeling sad, she would pull herself together and change the subject. At our tenth session she came into the office very assertively and said, "For the first time last night I started to look at my husband with just a little sense of compassion and there was a desire in my heart to understand him. I can't go there: he hurt me too much. If I keep working with you I may lose my anger toward him, so I'm terminating our sessions." She fired me.

Divorced, after being married for fifteen years, George said, "I don't even miss her. I'm surprised because I would have thought that after fifteen years of being together, shouldn't I feel something?" So was he grieving the loss of grief? Or was his heart blocked to the relationship so that when his wife left, it was out of sight, out of mind? Divorced from her husband for five years, a lady told me, "I keep on performing, but I've stopped living. You see me at church but I'm not there, you see me at work but I'm not there." She described the experience as if she were living in a daze.

Another phenomenon presenting itself is that people speak of feeling a painful sense of emptiness inside their hearts. A lady who held down a responsible job and was well educated said, "I don't know, but something has died inside me. I feel empty. Nothing seems to matter. I just go through the motions. I don't feel the way I used to feel years ago." In a similar light a well-known politician shared in a personal discussion, "I just don't have the passion for people I used to have years ago, something has changed within me. I just don't seem to care as much. I want to care and I know that I should be concerned, but I find myself in a distant situation where I seem divorced from the people who were once close to me."

Philip Cushman also noted this sense of emptiness:

It is possible to see evidence of this empty self in current psychological discourse about narcissism and borderline states. Popular culture's emphasis on consuming, political advertising strategies that emphasize soothing and charisma instead of critical thought, and a national difficulty in maintaining personal relationships.[2]

This situation is further enhanced by the pervasive conflict, or dare I say hatred, developing between parents and children. During the past three years I have had the opportunity to work with three young men ranging in age from 14 – 17 who categorically stated that if they had the chance, they would want to kill or hurt their fathers. They said their fathers were abusive to their mothers, callous, and indifferent. They found it almost impossible to trust their fathers' sincerity and being around them produced a sense of irritation, hostility, and disgust. What does this mean? Is it different from when we were growing up? Of course we would sometimes feel angry with our parents, but the thought of hurting them was foreign to us. What happened at Columbine in Colorado and the many incidents of childhood violence toward teachers and others give further food for thought, but the point I want to make is that we are facing a crisis of intimacy in what is becoming a distant world. We have increasingly sophisticated technologies for communication, yet we seem to be communicating less and becoming more isolated; at the same time we are trying to grope towards a global village. This poem describes it well:

> There is a coldness in the world
> That was not here before;
> One sees it in the sky,
> One feels it in the air,
> The trees, though root the same,
> Are somewhere far away
>
> There is a coldness in the world
> That was not here before;
> Is something in the wizened night,
> The stars, though shining,
> Are not bright,

The moon, though fresh positioned,
Is not new.

There is a coldness in the world
That was not here before;
The climes of season tell,
Spring flowers, though open,
Do not bloom,
And summer's timely fruit,
Fail to ripe,
And winter's virgin snow,
Is not white.

There is a coldness in the world
That was not here before;
One sees it in the people's eyes,
As foreigners passing by,
The mothers, through birth,
Do not give,
The children, though sparrows,
Do not sing,
The church bell, though tolling,
Does not tell.

From where comes this coldness in the world
That was not here before?
From where the dying,
From where the old,
From where the sunless day,
From where the boring night?
Where goes the heart from love,
And beauty from its sight?
Who closed this stable door,
For all the rich and all the poor,
Thought blanketed,
Still shivering.[3]

SPIRITUALITY AND INTIMACY

Intimacy is one facet of spirituality. The Latin root *spiritus* means life force, basic energy, being or breath of life, inspiration. Represented in many languages, the concept of spirit as breath in Hebrew is *ruaah*, in Greek *pneuma* and in Sanskrit *prajna*. Spirituality, like breathing, is deeply intimate. Definitions sometimes blur the essence of what we seek to describe, but spirituality in broad terms may be defined as a life style—conscious or unconscious—that involves ultimate belief (in God, Jesus Christ or a Higher Power) as it relates to the evolution of personal meaning, the development of community, and the informed caring or concern for God's garden, the world. Similarly, intimacy is the inward state involving the deepest relationship with ultimate reality—the self, others and the environment. One may argue, then, that the breakdown of intimacy we see around us may have a lot to do with the lack of emphasis on the development of spirituality in our modern world. During my years as a visiting professor at Yale Divinity School, Henri Nouwen, a deeply spiritual person committed to prayer, made a deep impression on me. According to Nouwen, "The intimacy of a house of love always leads to a solidarity with the weak, the closer we come to the heart of the One who loves us with an unconditional love, the closer we come to each other in the solidarity of a redeemed humanity."[4]

Spirituality may be divided into devotional and contemplative perspectives. *Devotional spirituality* invites God to be the guest in our life, while we still hold the reigns and call the shots. The emphasis is on doing things to please or placate God as the basis of our faith. The end result is a works-based belief focusing on *doing* rather than *being*. Tragically we tend to become human doings rather than human beings. This focus on doing fits into the hustle and bustle of modern culture, where we live under enormous time pressures, dehumanizing competition, and an almost unbearable burden to achieve at any cost. Devotional spirituality in many ways reflects the market culture of today. It also motivates the emphasis on prosperity religion—which believes that the more we serve God, the greater our material reward.

Contemplative spirituality invites God into our life as a guest, but then recognizes the lordship of God. We bow in worship by turning over the reigns of our lives so that God becomes the host—Lord of all.

Contemplation is a deep form of spirituality in which we commit to the intention of allowing God's presence and action in our lives. Going against the grain of our modern society, with all its hustle and bustle, contemplative spirituality calls us to the importance of silence in waiting for the guidance of God through the Holy Spirit. The focus here is on being, rather than doing. This does not mean that in contemplative spirituality we become lazy and refuse to do, but that the fire of God's love burning in our hearts expresses itself in our wanting to show love and caring for those around us and for the environment. In devotional spirituality the temptation is to make ourselves the center of activity, whereas contemplative spirituality calls us to wait in silence for God and God alone. In contemplative spirituality our activity originates in God and is led by God and not by ourselves. Contemplation enables a growing transformation of consciousness, manifested by a life that is lived from the source of love—our true selves in God, and expressed to our fellow beings and the world around us. According to Thomas Merton, "Contemplation is the highest expression of man's intellectual and spiritual life. It is that life itself fully awake, fully active, fully aware that it is alive ... it is spontaneous awe at the sacredness of life, of being."[5]

Freud used the concept of the psyche, but I find in my work with people in different parts of the world that the heart seems to be a warmer and more accessible concept. What is the heart? Obviously I do not mean the physical organ, but from medieval times the heart has been a metaphor for the center of our being. It is the place where love and hate co-exist. It is the decision-making center where all our choices—good and evil—are decided. It is the part of ourselves where we relate to the beautiful and the ugly, the holy and the profane. The heart is both conscious and unconscious. In a sense the heart is a universe within—as wide as the heavens above with all the stars and planets. In essence intimacy and spirituality are really all about the heart. The Bible warns us to guard our heart because out of it flows the issues of our life (Proverbs 4:23). This is an ancient saying but so hard for us to absorb. The reality is that most of our issues come from within us, and it takes a lot of courage to realize that persons or situations outside our control do not cause them. But this is also very hopeful, because the only person we can work with or change is our self. In essence then, the issues of spirituality and intimacy are very personal and everyone has to make their own decisions. This is not to minimize the role of external circumstances in our lives—for example, growing up in a drug infested area can have a powerful effect on the choices a child will make. In contemplation, life loses its opaqueness and becomes transparent to allow us to experience the events of our life as pathways rather than obstacles to the fullness of living.

The heart is also a place of understanding and reasoning. According to Pascal, "The heart has reasons that the mind knows not of."[6] The heart functions in love but it is also the reservoir of our anger and hurt. And so the heart, like a sponge, can become so filled with anger and hurt that there is no space left for love: love might be hitting us over the head like a piece of wood, but still our hearts cannot experience it. Hence one reason for the lack of intimacy in the modern world is that many of us have allowed our hearts to become filled with the hurt and anger of past years, making it very difficult to open up to intimacy with ourselves, each other and our environment. According to Merton, the heart is the deepest psychological ground of our personality, the inner sanctuary where self-awareness goes beyond analytical reflection and opens into metaphysical and theological confrontation with the abyss of the *unknown yet present*—one who is more intimate to us then we are to ourselves.[7]

Wherever you are, you are what's missing! In other words, the issues of life relate to what is going on inside us. Projection is one of the oldest human defenses. Remember Adam? When God asked him what went wrong, Adam blamed Eve. When God confronted Eve, she blamed the helpless serpent. But of course when the serpent's time came, he didn't have a leg to stand on!

The challenge of intimacy, like the challenge of contemplation, is to make the journey to our hearts, to the place where we truly exist. In essence contemplation and intimacy mean living from the heart. But this is not as easy as it seems. As the Bahamian saying goes, "I've been to Nassau, I've been to Abaco, I've been to Harbor Island, but I've never been to me." Tragically many of us live and die without experiencing more than half of the depth of our hearts.

Rosemary was a very attractive young lady of twenty-six. Lonely, isolated, and shy, she had no social life. She told me: "I hate my life." Suffering from tuberculosis as a young girl, she had to be isolated, which produced a feeling of being unwanted and rejected, giving her a negative view of herself. As a result she felt nobody would ever love her. Rosemary was totally self-absorbed, avoiding people, and extremely co-dependent. As she worked in therapy, Rosemary became less defensive and more assertive. Moving from a passive-aggressive stance, she began to express her anger openly, especially towards me and other people in her life. As she became more assertive even her posture changed. Paying more attention to looking after herself, Rosemary changed her hairstyle and make-up and became even more attractive. As her therapy continued, to my surprise, she shared with me that she had met a young man. Some time later they started playing tennis together and had lots of fun because whoever lost a point had to give the other person a back rub. This continued for a while and then the back rub changed to a kiss. Eventually she was able to express intimately her deep love towards the young man. By first becoming intimate with herself, Rosemary was able to be intimate with her friend. This was paralleled by a deep spirituality and involvement in her church. The healing of our hearts confronts all the dimensions of our lives—physical, spiritual, emotional, and social.

THE LAST SUPPER

This is one of the most intimate stories in all of scripture, portraying our Lord sharing a very close time with his disciples. The painting of the Last Supper by Leonardo da Vinci has a special story attached to it. Gaetano, my friend from Italy, told me that it took Leonardo da Vinci about twenty years to finish the painting because he could not find a model for Judas. Finally he came across a man who he felt would fit the part. Approaching the man he said, "Sir, would you consider being a model for Judas in the painting of the Last Supper?" The man replied, "Maestro, don't you remember me, don't know you who I am? Twenty years and a lifetime ago you chose me to model for your painting of Jesus."[8] The wounds of life have a way of affecting not only our hearts but also our appearances. The Last Supper (John 13-17) was a powerful statement of contemplation and intimacy as Christ was saying goodbye to his disciples before going to his mission on the cross. The process of termination is very important in psychotherapy because often feelings are heightened and we are open to hear messages of life-changing wisdom. The Last Supper illustrates seven qualities, which I think integrate contemplation and intimacy; these may help us in our own journey toward authenticity and love. They are love, communion, resistance, humility, simplicity, service, and transcendence.

Love

Expressing the deepest form of love, Jesus said to his disciples, "As the Father has loved me, so have I loved you" (John 15:9). Contemplation and intimacy emanate from love, and our Lord reminds us that his love reaches out to us in the most despairing and difficult points of our life. This is especially meaningful because it challenges us to seek to live a life of love:

> Many waters cannot quench love;
> rivers cannot wash it away.
> If one were to give
> all the wealth of his house for love,
> it would be utterly scorned. (Song of Solomon 8:7)

Regardless of how much we may have failed, how fallen we have become, or how much we feel like outcasts, Jesus reminds us that we are loved. Contemplation is opening ourselves to the deep love of God, which restores the meaning of our identity. Contemplation is the experience of living from the heart, of accepting that God loves us as we are. Contemplation enables us to experience something of our true selves by the melting away of our false selves, our defenses. This is discussed further in chapter 4. No one gives up on their false self unless they are loved. Opening ourselves to God's love in contemplation, and realizing that we are loved to the uttermost, enables us to move beyond our false, defensive selves (chapter 5). We open up to God's love in our true selves; the love that will never let us go, and the face that never turns away. Intimacy involves opening up to the love of God while contemplation involves coming to a deep, liberating realization that our identity, above all else, is based on being a person beloved by God. Basking in the warm sunshine of God's love we move beyond our inauthentic selves to our true selves as the beloved of God (chapter 6). In this process our small I is swallowed up by the great I am and as a result we live in God and he lives in us; then we can hear the words of God to Abraham, "Do not be afraid, Abram. I am your shield, your very great reward" (Genesis 15: 1). Contemplation means coming to accept that what we seek is not the consolation of God, but God himself—who is our consolation.

The love of God starts, maintains, and completes the spiritual journey. According to Nouwen, the spiritual journey involves three basic movements. [9] The first is the movement from loneliness to solitude. Loneliness is isolation, but solitude is being alone with the Alone.a Solitude is meaningful in that it prepares us to form true community in our relationships. Without solitude, instead of creating a healing community, we form a crowd. Without true community based on solitude we experience loneliness. The second movement of the spiritual life is from hostility to hospitality. Life is wounded. Many of us have within ourselves a powerful hurt trail involving aspects of abandonment, rejection, humiliation, guilt, and shame. As a result it is very easy to allow our hearts to become filled with all the anger and hurt of our lives, leaving no space for love. As we open our lives through working on ourselves in therapy or a deep prayer life, we empty ourselves of hurt and anger creating in our hearts a loving place where we can be at one with God, each other, and ourselves. There is no true emptying of the heart without grieving. Drawing people together, grieving enhances intimacy. Christ said, "Blessed are those who mourn, for they will be comforted" (Matthew 5:4). Yet because of the losses we have experienced, many of us stay at the grievance pole, that is the anger pole, rather than processing our grief and moving on. Full of anger, we may feel empowered but our anger prevents us from taking advantage of the love that exists around us.

The third movement of the spiritual life is from illusion to prayer. Stuck in our false selves we become drowned in selfishness or narcissism, which creates elusive programs for so-called happiness involving such things as our possessions, idolatries, addictions, consumerism, and perfectionism (chapter 4). But as we open our hearts to work through the anger and hurt in our lives, our false selves melt away and we experience love in our true selves from God who is always within us. God is the real and all that is real. He leads us from an illusive, destructive lifestyle to the experience of being beloved by him. We cannot develop our true selves without opening our hearts in prayer to empty ourselves of our false selves, with their false values and false identities. In essence then, moving beyond the powerful hurt trails of our lives and accepting that we can be loved, is made possible by experiencing afresh the reality that God loves us to the uttermost: the love that will never let us go and the face that never turns away.

Communion

The disciples were having a time of communion, a time of deep, pleasant fellowship. The spiritual journey at its heart is really all about communion, communion with God, ourselves, others, and the world around us. The essence of the gospel is that God loves us and is always seeking communion with us. He is always reaching out to us. He comes to us through nature—a beautiful sunset or sunrise; he reaches out to us through animals—a dog who shows us unconditional love; he touches us through a child's face—in a baby's face you can sometimes see the face of an angel; he sometimes reaches out to us in a sermon—giving us a peek into the glory of his presence, the joy of his love. But sadly because of the hurt in our hearts, we miss him. We just don't trust love anymore because where we expected love—in our home, family, or marriage—we received hurt and so in some sense we have closed the shutters of our lives to block out the pain and the garbage of our hurt. Sadly, however, whenever we close the shutters to block the view of the garbage, we also block out the gladioli, magnolias, and the beautiful bougainvillea. We cannot have sweet communion with a love who seeks us without being vulnerable. Oh Lord, help us to open up to your love.

Communion with God will always involve silence, "Be still, and know that I am God" (Psalm 46:10). Opening ourselves to external silence creates interior silence, and interior silence creates stillness, making space for God and ourselves to sit at the table set for two. "You prepare a table before me in the presence of my enemies" (Psalm 23:5). "Here I am! I stand at the door and knock. If anyone hears my voice and opens the door, I will come in and eat with him, and he with me" (Revelation 3:20). Experiencing the presence of God in silence is a discipline, a learning experience. David said, "I have stilled and quieted my soul; like a weaned child with its mother" (Psalm 131:2). In the silence of contemplation we open ourselves to the naked love of God's presence, which bathes our souls, creating the deepest form of intimacy and communion.

Resistance

In this beautiful environment of the Last Supper, all was not well. Judas was planning sabotage. There is always a Judas, and so often the Judas is us. Hurt and anger in our hearts makes us our own worst enemies and as a result we become experts at self-sabotage. This ability to be self-destructive is one of the commonest ways we create distance in our lives while at the same time destroying intimacy with God, others and ourselves. Analyzing this, Jesus admonishes us to love our enemies (Luke 6:35) because so often we are our own worst enemies. Contemplation or deep spirituality requires welcoming those difficult, resistant parts of our hearts to experience the deep understanding of God's love in our lives.

Resistance in our spiritual journey is usually associated with, if not caused by, anger. Much anger results from the effect of our repressed childhood trauma presenting itself in our adult lives. It may, of course, be provoked, but a person can only provoke the anger that is already in our hearts. Painful as it may seem, anger is a message from the heart to come home to ourselves: by facing and working through the hurt and anger in our hearts we open ourselves to the deep love of God. Through a ripple effect, this creates intimacy in the distant world around us. Anger is discussed in more detail in chapter 3.

Humility

Humility is the building block of spirituality and contemplation. It always leads to intimacy. In essence, humility is facing the truth about our lives: learning to accept ourselves as we actually are—not as we would like to be or feel we should be. Taking off his outer garment, our Lord took upon himself the garb of a slave to give himself in service to his disciples and wash their feet. As we open to God's love we have to be willing to allow God to expose our prejudices, our superior attitudes, our competitive jealousies, and our alienating tendencies. We then have to be willing to let go of them. Having its derivation from the Latin word humus which means soil, humility involves preparing the soil of our hearts to grow the seeds of God's love in our lives. I believe many of us have allowed our hearts to become hardened and it is difficult for the seeds of love to grow. This unplowed ground must be tilled by working through the very painful hurts and experiences of anger that so often characterize our deep inner selves. As we open our hearts to the presence of God in our lives, he creates fertile ground where the seeds of love can prosper.

Simplicity

Our Lord took a basin of water to wash his disciples' feet. At its heart life is simple. A lady dying of cancer said to me, "Dying is so easy, no long sermons, not much food to eat, no bills to pay, just waiting for it to happen." But then, after being healed, she became vulnerable to the powerful consumerism surrounding our lives. She bought a house with increasing bills and said, "I wish I could live in health as I lived when I was dying." I will never forget what she said, looking me straight in the face: "David, at its heart, life is very simple but we spend so much of our life making it complex." We defend ourselves against the triangle of hurt involving abandonment, rejection, and humiliation by making life complex: living beyond our means, working too hard, not making the right choices, not exercising. As our lives become more and more complex, so it becomes more difficult for us to be aware of the presence of God's love. The basin of water is a very powerful picture of simplicity. Let us be reminded that as parents our kids want us, not what we can give them; let us be reminded that people seek contact with us, and not necessarily what we can offer them.

Obviously, simplifying our lives in this very complex society is easier said than done, but it seems to me that if we are going to journey along the experience of contemplation, spirituality, and intimacy, we have to travel lighter. This may mean some very hard choices, but these very choices can dictate the quality and experience of the love that we so desire. One gentleman was offered a special job traveling around the world to sell a product. The pay was excellent and the job would help to further his career, but recognizing that the increased fatigue and stress involved would interfere with his contemplative prayer experience, he turned the job down. He said that the job was good for his career but terrible for his vocation. It is important to stress that the opportunities to simplify our lives seem to occur at specific times; at certain points simplification is much easier than at other times. If we do not take advantage of these opportunities we can find ourselves entering a greater sense of complexity. Nothing, and I say nothing, is more painful than to realize that one is caught up into a vortex of the hustle and bustle of life—virtually running in circles and yet having no time or space to be present to one's self. So many of us, including myself, have lived this life. Such lives put us further and further away from the God who loves us and calls us to himself, but worse than that, they really lead us away from who we are, from each other, and from the world around us.

Service

Dressed as a slave, our Lord bowed and washed his disciples' feet. What a paradox, the Holy Almighty God washing the feet of ordinary, lowly human beings. This and this alone is God's love, providing a beautiful picture of contemplation and intimacy. Though the Lord God is high and mighty, his love is always towards those who are humble and contrite. This foot wash-ing demonstrates the love which never fails us, a love which reminds us that Christ still washes our feet by sending us friends to encourage us, children to admire us, and spouses to love us. The story does not end there because when Jesus came to wash Peter's feet, Peter objected, but Jesus in a very simple way implied to Peter that if he refused to let his feet be washed then in some sense he was choosing not to belong. Many of us are very good at giving, but have a very hard time receiving love. Contemplation means not just the giving of love but also a deep apprecia-tion and the receiving of love. It involves saying sincerely from the heart, "Thank you," or "I appreciate you." What a revolution might occur if we learnt to express our gratitude and appreciation more freely to our chil-dren, to our spouses, to those who work with us. Thankfulness has a way of cleansing the air and creating a loving, open community.

Coming to Judas, Christ looked into his eyes and spoke inaudibly (that is without words), "Judas, you don't need to do this. Even right now we can work it out". But oh, the hardness of the heart! When the false self forms onion-like layers around the heart, the hurt triangle of abandonment, rejection, and humiliation becomes so intractable that our hearts become like stone and even though love may be very close to us, staring us in the face, it is very difficult for us to open our hearts to receive it. We don't have to live this way, we don't have to destroy ourselves, we can stop and change. I believe Jesus washed Judas' feet most carefully of all. This to me is a very powerful lesson; love is not just getting along with those who appreciate us, but in a very deep sense contemplative spirituality means moving in love even toward those who would use or reject us.

In this modern age many of us are tired, working extremely hard, and stressed with many pressures: we need our feet washed. How important it is to wash each other's feet. This may be literally or figuratively—a kind word, an encouraging hug, a letter or phone call. The fact is that we all need to wash each other's feet. As Jesus said, "Now that I, your Lord and Teacher, have washed your feet, you also should wash one another's feet" (John 13:14).

Transcendence

Jesus told his disciples that he was going away, but that when they received each other they would also be receiving him. How important it is in the spiritual journey to recognize that Jesus comes to us so often in other people. Contemplation is really living from the love of God embedded in our hearts; this allows us to see Christ in people around us. Contemplation is recognizing Christ in the midst of life, in spite of all its hurt and pain, a transcendent reality touching us. What would happen today if we could see our child as Jesus? What would happen today if we could see our wife as Jesus? What would happen today if we could see our husband or our best friend as Jesus coming to us and saying, "I want to love you"? My point is that if this happens, something will change in our ability to be open to intimacy. Jesus is the lover who always seeks the beloved: he always comes. The tragedy is that because of the busyness in our lives, the fatigue in our hearts, and the resistance in our minds we often miss the awareness of his presence. Gertrude Stein was quoted as saying, "A rose is a rose is a rose." This is very true, but a rose is also a statement from God—booming to us in his loving voice that we are loved. In other words, as we open our hearts to the transcendent and imminent presence of God, we begin to see his presence in everything around us: he is in the roses, the children, the adults, ourselves and all of life. The ordinary becomes the bearer of the extraordinary.

It was a Tuesday morning; she was about eighty years old. Coming into my office she was deeply hurt. Although it was a very bright, sunlit morning, the pain in this dear old lady's face was such that it seemed to darken the room; I could see that something serious was taking place in her life.

She looked at me and said, "Dr. Allen, I'm only here because of a friend who read your book, *In Search of the Heart*. She told me to come and see you before I killed myself. I am experiencing something that is so difficult I know I can't cope with it and I feel the only way out is to kill myself. I have bought a gun and I plan to shoot myself." She continued, "I have been in a church for many years, I have even been a missionary, I've raised children and grandchildren. But," she said, "this is the first time in my life that I have met pain that is bigger than me. If I were a younger lady, I could handle it. I could leave my husband and perhaps start over fresh, but at my age I do not have the finances and there is no way I could start up again. I see no way out but to kill myself even though I am a believer. I will have to bargain with God because this pain is just bigger than I can bear."

Without going into details, her problem could be summed up as the destruction of fifty years of trust. She said, "I believe in God. I love God. But there's just no way I can live with this kind of pain." She was very clear in her own mind, saying, "There's no drug you can give me to help me, in fact there's nothing you can say to help me, I'm only here because my friend asked me to come, and so I am being faithful to her." The pathos and the pain in the dear lady's face affected my heart and after listening to her for quite a while, I began to ask her about her faith and if it had anything to say to her at a time like this. She spoke very clearly about her faith but said that the pain was greater than anything she had ever experienced. I then challenged her as to whether she had thought of the cross as a means of maintenance in daily life, and not only as a means of salvation. I tried to make the point that the reality, in spite of the pain she was experiencing, was that Jesus was able to carry that pain on the cross and she did not have to carry it herself. As Isaiah said, "Surely he took up our infirmities and carried our sorrows" (Isaiah 53:4). By allowing Christ to carry her pain on the cross she could be relieved and experience healing in her heart. I could see she thought that this was rather simplistic.

We worked together for about three months and I noticed that each week she seemed to be getting stronger. We talked particularly about the process of allowing Christ to carry our pain in the present and not just seeing our faith as something that was experienced on Sunday and irrelevant to the pathos of our everyday pain. After three months I felt that she had made so much progress that we should take a break in our work.

I suggested one final weekly session, then monthly sessions just to see how things were going.

At the next session she surprised me by coming in carrying a large bag with pieces of wood sticking out. The dear lady took out two crosses and explained, "Dr. Allen, after our first session I went into the woods and collected some wood, then I went into my husband's workshop and I made two crosses, this big one and this small one." They were not very attractive, neither were they well made, but there was something very, very special about these crosses. She said that she would like to leave them with me "because maybe other people will come into your office with experiences like mine. Keep these crosses in your office so that when people come in crushed by pain, you can tell them the story of the old lady. After I made them, I put them in the corner of my room and each day I would share with Christ that I couldn't carry this pain but he would have to carry it for me on the cross. And I want to let you know, Dr. Allen, that he did."

I keep one of the crosses in my room at home and the other in the office. I have since had the chance to present the cross and tell the story of the old lady to many different types of people and couples coming to the office feeling hopeless and in despair. It is amazing to see people who were extremely hostile break down in tears as they open to the simple story of the old lady and the cross. As the old hymn says: "To the old rugged cross, I will ever be true." How important to recognize that when we face the pains and the crises of life, God loves us and carries our burdens and sorrows. "Come to me, all you who are weary and burdened, and I will give you rest" (Matthew 11:28).

CONCLUSION

According to Henri Nouwen, "Contemplative prayer requires that we listen, that we let God speak to us when he wants and in the way he wants. This is difficult for us precisely because it means allowing God to say what we might not want to hear. But if we listen long and deeply, God will reveal himself to us, as a soft breeze or a still small voice; he will offer himself to us in gentle compassion."[10] As we come to know God intimately in our hearts, we reflect this to the world around us, allowing us to experience intimacy and unity in the midst of diversity. These themes are explored in the following chapters.

REFERENCES

1. Wallace Stevens, "The Relations Between Poetry And Paintings", *The Necessary Angel* (New York: Random, 1951), 3.
2. Philip Cushman, "Why the Self is Empty," *The American Psychologist* 45, no. 5 (May 1990), 599.
3. David Allen Jr, (unpublished).
4. Henri J.M. Nouwen, *Life Signs* (Garden City, New York: Doubleday, 1986), 51.
5. Thomas Merton, *New Seeds of Contemplation* quoted in *These Words Upon Your Heart* ed Paul Ofstedal (Minneapolis: Augsburch Fortress, 2002), 142.
6. Blaise Pascal, quoted in *Seeds of Peace* by William Shannon (New York: Crossword, 1996), 37.
7. Thomas Merton, *Contemplative Prayer* (New York: Doubleday, 1972), 33.
8. Gaetano Sottile, (personal communication).
9. Henri J. M. Nouwen, *Reaching Out: The Three Movements of the Spiritual Life* (Garden City, New York: Doubleday, 1986).
10. Henri J. M. Nouwen, *Clowning in Rome: Reflections on Solitude, Celibacy, Prayer, and Contemplation* (Garden City, New York: Doubleday, 1979), 106.

CHAPTER 2
SOULLESSNESS: THE MODERN NEMESIS

Soullessness keeps company with fear. People who have given up their souls have only a body and it is the body that they are terrified about. As a result they are afraid of losing the creature comforts that still remain. People who have not given up their souls can overcome fear because in the end fear always comes from within and not from without. (Ivan I. Klima[1])

In recent years, consultation with people from different parts of the world indicates an increasing phenomenon involving the sense of emptiness or poverty of the inner life. One attractive, well-dressed lady who appeared very urbane said, "My soul is dead." Having not heard of that concept before I asked her what she meant. She said that once she was very caring and sensitive. If she passed someone on the street who was in need, she was happy to stop and offer help. But now, she just feels cut off. "I don't feel connected, I just can't be bothered." Describing the situation further she said, "My heart has become cold and life has become an autonomous bore. I keep on going but I don't know why." I tried to discuss how she felt about this. As she began to express her feelings, she would say, "That's not rational," or "That doesn't make cognitive sense." It appeared that she reasoned away her feelings, but they remained and were even part of her reasoning. Her fear of her feelings drove her reason to dismiss her emotions, so she lived apart from her heart.

This experience does not fit into a classic psychiatric diagnosis, but it describes a sense of emptiness that is associated with feelings of disconnection within and without. Another person explained that she had learned to live apart from her heart because being sensitive, being vulnerable to the pain of life, took too much out of her. It was easier to live life more cognitively. In no way do I want to imply that these people were not caring, good human beings, but there seemed to be a powerful disconnection between their outer and inner lives.

Another young lady had a fairly happy relationship with her husband, but then things went sour and they were divorced. She put it this way: "Since the divorce I continue to perform but have stopped living. I can be at work, but a large part of me isn't there. I go to church, but I'm not really there. As a result I find myself cutting off from relationships and withdrawing from social groups I was once a part of. I'm not depressed or even sad, it's just that I can't be bothered."

Another gentleman who had been married for about twenty years claimed that he and his wife had traveled together and done many interesting and pleasant things, but then as time went on they grew apart and in his words, "fell out of love," and she went her way and he went his. What struck me was that he was not troubled about why the relationship broke up, but by his own lack of grief at loosing his wife of 20 years. He said, "I feel nothing. I feel empty. We had good times, there are some memories but I really haven't grieved the loss of her." In a sense he was grieving the loss of grief! We expect to grieve in certain situations but because our hearts are blocked we are unable to grieve so we grieve the loss of grief.

One spring morning I was having a time of quiet meditation in a small park in the greater Washington area; the tulips were in full bloom. They were just beautiful— purple, orange, red, and yellow; their splendor was magnificent. Entranced by their beauty I wanted to share my excitement. Stopping a passing gentleman I pointed out the tulips to him. With disgust in his voice he said, "Flowers! I have no time for flowers, I have to go to work." I was taken aback by his strong reaction that it was a waste of time looking at flowers. The rapid pace of our lives and the pressures upon us affect our ability to appreciate beauty. Of course I had no right to try to force on him my contemplative or spiritual experience of the flowers.

Jogging slowly in the Western part of Nassau, I was stunned by a beautiful sunset; it was absolutely splendid. I found myself thinking about getting a picture of it or somehow capturing it so that I could use it in a lecture. By the time I had considered all the options, the sunset was gone. Why did I have to consume the sunset? Why did I have to organize it or use it? Why couldn't I just be with the sunset and allow myself to be grasped by it? Sadly, during my life I've lost so many sunsets.

Soullessness, which is essentially intimacy dysfunction associated with pathological narcissism, is a catchall for many of the issues that eat at the heart and soul of modern life. After being hurt in an intimate relationship we may decide never to be close again. The danger is that whenever we refuse to be intimate, or to open our hearts to love, we build walls. These walls will hide the garbage but they also hide the beauty of the magnolias. As Tennyson said, "Tis better to have loved and lost than never to have loved at all."[2] In soullessness the inner life lacks love and compassion, and the appreciation of beauty is blocked, diminished, or destroyed. Soullessness may be acute, chronic, or long-term. In my experience, whenever I start the day in a rush, I am harried, unsettled, and running from appointment to appointment. I have come to realize that my daily experience is a constant fight against soullessness, a fight to live from my deeper self or inner life. Appreciating our inner lives takes time. It is not as easy as it seems because the pressures we live under encourage us to externalize our life and to forget we have a soul within. "What good is it for a man to gain the whole world, yet forfeit his soul?" (Mark 8:36) What can a person give in exchange for their soul? Each day we should see something beautiful, read some poetry, and have some good conversation to keep our hearts alive. Georgia O'Keefe summarized it neatly:

> No one sees a flower.
> No one makes a friend.
> To see a flower takes time.
> To make a friend takes time.
> And we have no time.[3]

The lack of time or attention to our inner lives causes a gradual dulling of our hearts and as a result it blocks our ability to be open to love, passion, and the appreciation of beauty.

Years ago, while visiting Prague and giving a lecture at the University of Charles, I came across the work of Ivan Klima, a survivor of the Holocaust.[4] Klima was a major contributor to the Velvet Revolution in which the communist government of the Czech Republic fell without force. In his words quoted at the beginning of the chapter, Klima stresses that soullessness keeps company with fear. He claims that people who have given up their souls have only a body and it is the body that they are terrified about. They are afraid of losing the creature comforts that still remain, for example, peace and quiet, material things, convenience, and luxuries. According to Klima, people who have not given up their souls can overcome fear because they know that in the end fear always comes from within and not from without. Our modern state of emptiness has also been described by the well-known Bahamian psychologist, Dr. Timothy McCartney, "Belly full but soul empty."[5] Committed to a powerful consumerism to supply the physical comforts of life, we are left with a haunting emptiness in our inner lives.

CAUSES OF SOULLESSNESS

When we deal with the heart we face mystery and it is hard to be concrete, so it may be more appropriate to talk about associations than causes.

Family Breakdown

In modern society one of the major issues facing us is the break down of the nuclear and extended family, affecting the bonding of children to their parents; our children are more isolated and in some sense may have to use their psychological energy to cope with life rather than to experience the beauty around them. To the extent that a child does not internalize the love of a parent, this child will have difficulty loving and grieving—the two being closely interconnected. As the child grows older they feel empty within and it is difficult to connect or to be intimate with others. This emptiness may be filled by ambitious achievement or in more negative ways with drugs, sex, and violence. But no matter which way we look at it, the breakdown of the family in modern life is deeply associated with the concept of soullessness. Particularly noticeable is the breakdown of what is called the container model. Years ago the child was contained by the nuclear family, which was in turn contained by the extended family, the community, the church, the synagogue, and in some sense the town or city. In present society children are often not shielded from the pain of life because of the breakdown of the nuclear family, the distant separation of the extended family, the lack of bonded communities, and the lack of caring religious communities. As a result the modern child's intense exposure to pain forces upon them an adult experience, without the emotional and life knowledge to cope. Some of our children experience pain at 10-15 years of age that we did not have to face until we were in our 30s or 40s. These child adults, in later life, make up for their loss of childhood experience by becoming adult children. This is particularly seen in the field of alcoholism where adults from alcoholic families are known as adult children of alcoholics.

I will never forget a young lady describing her father pointing a gun at her mother when she was 10 years old. She said that something broke within her, and since then her life had been filled with fear and uncertainty, making it hard for her to maintain a long-term loving relationship. Such experiences have a deleterious effect on a child's inner life, creating painful emptiness and resulting in a spiritual vagabond who drifts from relationship to relationship.

Disconnection

Another issue that is puzzling, and may be related to soullessness, is the disconnection or separation taking place between children and society. The recent happenings of Columbine and the increasing incidences of childhood violence in our culture may be indicative of an underlying malaise. What is their violent behavior saying? Is it saying they don't feel they belong to us or with us? Or maybe we don't know how to belong to them? But one thing is clear, we don't know how just to be, and so the destruction continues.

Busyness

The extreme busyness of modern society is associated with, or enhances, soullessness. As we move here and there in the hustle and bustle of life, we have no time for the inner life. We don't have time to reflect on our thoughts or our feelings and as a result we lose our ability to be human. We become human doings rather than human beings. This pressured life has been neatly summarized: "I have a great life but I don't know if I have time to show up for it." Soullessness means we are not showing up for our life to listen to the inner voice of love deep within ourselves, letting us know that we are the beloved of God.

Addictive tendencies

In Freud's time repression was the major issue of the day, but in the modern world things are very different. We still have some repression, but in many ways life is very unrepressed—sexuality, religion, or what have you. Our issues today tend to be more of attachment. We become attached to things that make us feel better about ourselves—money, family, drugs, self-absorption, power, or perfectionism. Connected to all of this is a very powerful advertising media, which in some sense controls modern culture. The advertising media creates an aura of psychological fusion attaching basic human drives or appetites for food and sex to material things. For example, buy the beer get the girl. Or a car advertisement where a quiet, soothing, almost sensuous sound of music with a candle-lit atmosphere makes us feel intimate or sexual but in the midst of all this a car appears. The subliminal message being—buy the car and it will open you up to the sexuality that you desire. Consumerism has a powerful affect on our lives. Going to the mall has been described as not going to look for something to buy, but going to look for something to want, something to fill the void.

Technology

The burgeoning technological revolution also affects our inner lives. People working in the same or adjacent offices may communicate more by e-mail than by verbal conversation. The loss of face-to-face communication and the art of conversation, which involve 'reading' an individual's face or body as well as their words, affect our hearts—leading to dehumanization.

Religion

Sometimes very strict religious tradition, which emphasizes ritual as opposed to personal expression or acceptance, makes the religious experience empty and soulless. The person becomes, as it were, an automaton going along with the tradition or the ritual but their heart or soul is not involved. This also leads to emptiness and a loss of the ability to love and appreciate beauty.

The false self

The development of the false self, a defense against our childhood hurts, creates illusive emotional programs for happiness that involve addictions, idolatries, self-absorption, pathological narcissism, perfectionism, and issues of power and control (chapter 4). It is appropriate for children to live in a fantasyland to protect themselves from the fears of abandonment, rejection, and shame, but the tragedy is that on reaching the age of self-reflective consciousness, because society does not honor the grieving process, many of us do not go back to do the grief work of our early childhood trauma. As a result, our false mind-made selves, which were once protective and somewhat a blessing for us in childhood, becomes more entrenched in later life. So our false selves become our functional selves and we begin the journey toward inauthenticity. The less authentic we are, the less we are able to be true to our inner lives, and so we become open to soullessness. Our false selves would do anything to prevent us from facing our true selves, but they are perverse rescuers, because when we face our pain we also open ourselves to joy. At the end of the false-self dynamic is the intense competitive spirit so common in our society; even at kindergarten level parents compete viciously to get their kids placed in the right schools so they can end up at the right colleges. This powerful competitive attitude eats away at our ability to feel compassion and love and to appreciate beauty.

SYMPTOMATOLOGY OF SOULESSNESS

Soullessness is characterized by a number of phenomena, which read rather like the symptoms of an illness. Despite these similarities, soullessness is not, of course, a medical condition.

Narcissism

One hallmark of soullessness is a strong pathological narcissism, an extreme self-absorption that makes it difficult to establish intimacy or community. Soulless people are generally on the take, with little desire to reciprocate. As one lady said, "I've given up inviting people over because they just don't reciprocate." Relationships must always be mutual if there's going to be meaningful growth. Soullessness is also characterized by a powerful manipulative tendency involving selfish ambition, with such a competitive killer instinct that we would virtually step on another person to get ahead. Students at certain medical schools described such a competitive atmosphere, that people stooped to stealing each other's lab results in order to get ahead. Lying or telling tales to hurt another's position at work is a similar phenomenon. This can be very painful, but in highly competitive situations it is the rule of the day; as a result, trust is very difficult to maintain. Note that this situation does not come about overnight, but subtly and often covertly.

Pathological narcissism is also seen in marriage where one of the spouses may be totally selfish and unwilling to give. An example of this concerned an artist who developed a very interesting product and was approached by an international art dealer who wanted to buy her work. Excited and rather overwhelmed, she asked her accountant husband to help her with the economics of pricing her work. Jealous of his wife's art and the success of her creativity, the husband refused to help her and as a result she lost the deal. Pleading with her husband for help, she was met by absolute refusal. This couple showed deep love for each other in other contexts, but over this issue what I call almost demonic competition occurred, and any resemblance of the inner life relating to love, compassion, and beauty was destroyed.

In the ancient Jewish Book of Esther, Haman—who was prime minister of the Persian Empire—demonstrated powerful signs of narcissism and soullessness. Moving up very fast in the king's court, Haman hated Mordecai, Esther's uncle, who had saved the king from a conspiracy against his life. To reward Mordecai the king asked Haman to design a suitable honor for a person who had done something really notable for the king. Haman's pathological narcissism led him to believe that the honor was for himself, so he suggested being seated on one of the king's horses and paraded around the city to receive the accolades and acclaim of the people. Totally narcissistic, the prime minister told the king who said, "A great idea, we'll do it. Tell Mordecai, and you can lead the horse." You can imagine the shock on Haman's face as he realized that he had designed an honor for the hated Mordecai.

Inability to grieve

Deep self-absorption makes us unable to grieve. As I mentioned earlier, I believe that we can only love as deeply as we can grieve and we all have different childhoods, and internalized the love of our parents to differing degrees. As a result some people have difficulty with the grieving process. Contributing to this, of course, is the cultural difference between men and women; in general women seem able to express their grief more easily than men. Grieving is a healing feeling that empties the heart. Over the years aborted grief reactions or unaddressed grief experiences cause our hearts to harden with hurt. A hardened heart is like a bucket of dry earth. If we pour water on the soil it sits on top without soaking in. This is a metaphor for soullessness. A person's heart can become so hard and resistant that even though bathed in or surrounded by love, the love cannot penetrate. Coping with loss is very difficult. All life involves change, all change involves loss, and all loss involves pain. It is only at the point of pain, if we do our grief work, that we can open ourselves to our love story. Without grief it is really hard to empty our hearts of pain, and therefore our hearts become hardened making it difficult to experience the inner life. A common sign of aborted grief reactions is that we tend to live more in the false self, preventing the formation of true community and meaningful solitude, resulting in a superficial form of living that makes it very difficult to connect and communicate. Intelligent, creative, and competent in many fields, we might write a good paper or present a spirited lecture, but our emotional connections are superficial or nonexistent because the ability to grieve is intimately related to the ability to love.

Lack of commitment

Another major symptom of soullessness is the lack of commitment seen in our culture. Commitment is the joining of two inner lives so there is a unity of the inner life—love, compassion, and appreciation of beauty. But it is really hard for us to commit. As one young lady said, "I just don't see how I can commit myself to one person for a lifetime, it just doesn't make sense to me." Soullessness makes long-term commitment to people and community more and more difficult. This has many implications for art, culture, and our communities. Some things take time, as Reinhold Niebuhr said, "Anything that is worth doing well requires more than a lifetime, therefore we need to live by hope."[6] In soullessness we find it difficult to wait, we find it difficult to have a long-term perspective; we want everything now. We take shortcuts—and the classic shortcut is the addiction process. Ideally satisfaction, fulfillment, and meaning in life result from hard work, a job well done, and the maturing experiences of life. But the hurt within our hearts propels us to seek a shortcut to the sense of fulfillment or high by seeking pleasure or avoiding pain in certain activities to which we become attached or addicted. These include drugs, sex, pleasing others (co-dependency), and money. In essence addiction removes the long-term perspective and makes us seek immediate gratification. It promises relief but in the end gives us pain.

Addiction

A person can lose a sense of who they really are through addiction. Their identity then becomes the addictive object. For example, John is a man and his problem is cocaine. Through the addictive process his identity becomes cocaine, and his problem becomes John. This powerful attachment to the addictive object leaves the person empty and soulless. A chronic cocaine addict looking at his life saw himself as a little boy. Recognizing the possibilities and opportunities that could have been, he was shocked and, although he was doing well in the program, said, "I've come this far in treatment, but the mountain ahead is so huge, I just don't see how I can go forward. I can never be like I was before this addiction, I just don't know how to do it." Within a short time he left the program saying, "I guess I'll just stick with cocaine." It's a hard reality, but the truth is that we tend to become what we are addicted to, and so often our choices define us.

Indifference

Another major symptom of soullessness is what I call "callous indifference" where a person can walk by someone who is hurting and not feel connected—not feel anything. Referring back to the Book of Esther, Prime Minister Haman was able to persuade the King to sign an edict to annihilate the Jews. When this dreadful news was announced, the Jews were horrified and feared for their lives. The story of Esther reports that after the Jews heard this pronouncement and were in turmoil, Prime Minister Haman sat down with the King and enjoyed a drink! He portrayed a total disconnection and lack of empathic concern for those around him. Callous indifference can also lead to violence—without empathic connection we are more likely to hurt those close to us.

Lying

A little-noticed effect of soullessness is the concept of lying, the white lie, which has become a common part of the fabric of our culture. We have a tendency to reconstruct reality to fit our situation. Two people reporting the same incident have a totally different perception or presentation of the situation. In soullessness a person has no difficulty reconstructing reality, or lying, to fit whatever makes him either feel better or suits the occasion. A busy young doctor had a severe addiction to narcotics, which he realized was putting his life and practice in danger. When it was suggested that he seek help, he replied, "I want to get help but I'm too busy building my practice and I can't afford to take the time off." These days it is also called spin. This relates to the concept of pathological narcissism discussed earlier. In the book of Esther, Prime Minister Haman was asked to develop an honor for Mordecai, who had saved the King's life, but Haman's pathological narcissism caused him to reconstruct reality to believe that he would be honored. He designed the honor for himself only to be in shock when he found out the king meant it for the man he hated, Mordecai.

Jealousy

Another symptom of soullessness is what I call hypersensitive jealousy. This is a very complex phenomenon, but I have seen it over and over. It occurs, for example, where a husband loses trust and suspects that his wife is having an affair. He hires a private investigator to check on her, but then loses trust in the private investigator, and hires another private investigator to check on the first. So the trend continues. In another incident a husband totally distrusted his wife and would not allow her to go out, keeping her a prisoner in the house. There are cases where a husband would literally check the bed or under the bed because he believed in his heart that his wife was being unfaithful. In my experience, even though one tries to be rational in discussing the situation, the belief is concrete and hard to dislodge.

Another example involved a distinguished doctor who had an affair with a younger woman, but feared that a young man would take her from him. He felt so anxious and insecure that when he left work he would follow the lady home to make sure she did not stop to see anyone. To make matters worse, he would wake in the night thinking that she might be out with someone else and would get up and drive around to her apartment to see if her car was there. If it were not, he would drive around the city looking for her. After a while he approached me and said, "I can't live like this, it's killing me. If I keep this up I will lose my practice and my reputation and everything I possess, I have to let the situation go." Worn out and burnt-out, he was eventually able to let go.

Hypersensitive jealousy seems to be associated with triangular relationships involving anger, intimacy, and depression. These three issues together produce a very destructive paranoia, which can result in serious violence and destruction. It can occur where two couples are very friendly and then something happens to create distance in the relationship. The incident is magnified and one spouse or partner acts in a pathologically jealous way. Paradoxically, the people we love the most tend to evoke the most anger in us.

Repression of beauty

Connected to the sense of the inner emptiness or void is what Rollo May described as the repression of beauty. "And beauty passes ever out of reach, save in the heart where happiness is home. There beauty walks wherever it may be and paints the setting of the sun on a quiet sea."[7] To appreciate beauty we have to first accept ourselves and have a sense of peace in our hearts. When we are upset either with our home, our family, or our job we can pass a beautiful mountain, a calm lake, or a beautiful flower and not really see it because our hearts are in turmoil or are just empty. The repression of beauty becomes a very powerful theme of the soulless life. This is terrible because in order to be fully alive we must occasionally hear the singing of angels, we must see that life rings with beauty: in a flower, in a baby's face, in the mountains and the oceans. Without this, life becomes banal—the rainbow just a collection of dust particles reflecting light, the beautiful aquamarine Bahamian sea just salt water.

The repression of beauty leads to a loss of excitement and enthusiasm so that ordinary living creates the painful state of boredom so prominent in our culture. As a result we seek 'highs,' that will lift us out of boredom—like a party or shopping. Because of the poverty of the inner life we tend to have more recognition memory than evocative memory. We take our children to Disney World in July, then in August they complain that they have done nothing all summer! It is as if they can't evoke the experience of going to Disney World, they can only experience it by repeating it. When I worked in the area of drugs and families, I would stress to parents how important it is to accept that some days are boring. When the kids say, "We are bored," just admit, "Yes we are bored, let's all be bored together," because if we can really accept the boring times, we can also appreciate more exciting times. When we need excitement all the time, it is an indication that we have become soulless; we are experiencing the poverty of our inner lives.

The repression of beauty also relates to *addictive seeing*. For example, when a young child sees a flower, they see what is in front of them because the child does not yet have an internalized image of the flower in their head. As the child grows older and develops an internal image of the flower in their head, there is a tendency to be more attached to the image of the flower in the head and to pay less attention to the reality of the flower in front of them. And so, as we become adults, we become addicted to internal images—and blind to the beauty of the real world around us. We could study the flower, dissect it scientifically, and know its components in cognitive-scientific terms. But to be aware of beauty means that we have to be with the flower, feeling its petals, smelling its aroma, grasped by its beauty. Becoming one with the flower opens us to our deeper selves and to an awareness of our common creator. Another facet of this addiction to internal images makes us blind and unresponsive to our life partners—we relate more to the internal images in our heads than to the people we live with.

"Holy, holy, holy is the Lord Almighty; the whole earth is full of his glory."(Isaiah 6:3) Herbert Read put it this way, "... the same forces that have destroyed the mystery of holiness have destroyed the mystery of beauty."[8] There is a vital connection between the vertical concept of worship and holiness, and the horizontal concept of the glory of God reflected in the beauty in the earth. Life without worship or holiness leaves us soulless and ungrateful. We feel that we deserve everything and everything we earn is ours—we forget that life itself is a grace; even the air we breathe is a gift. Our hearts becomes hardened, making us angry, ungrateful, and tenaciously possessive.

Technology

Technological efficiency may be an associated cause of soullessness but it is also a symptom of soullessness. The poverty of the inner life may be manifested by an over-commitment to technological efficiency or *vice versa*. For example, we spend our evenings and free time on a computer using e-mail and instant messaging, instead of putting time and effort into relationships with those around us. Often the soulless person has a powerful affinity for a technological lifestyle, finding it easier than being with real people, and dealing with real life. This is not to say that these technologies cannot be very useful and valuable, for example when communicating with an editor several time zones away! However, the technology can easily take over a person's life.

At the root of all these symptoms or characteristics lies the loss of a sense of the awe and mystery of life. As a result there is no true worship, prayer is nonexistent and we are left to become our own god. The soulless person, with a sense of emptiness, callous indifference, ingratitude, and anger, becomes blocked from really praying for another person. Prayer is relational and so if our hearts are blocked or we have intimacy dysfunction, our prayer life is also affected.

TREATMENT OF SOULLESSNESS

The answer to the problem of soullessness is complex, but there are five areas that may help us to grow our souls.

Connections

Relationships with other individuals are vital for the inner life to grow. The person I mentioned at the beginning of the chapter who described her soul as dead, spent four years in a group working on her communication and relationship issues. After a period of time her emotions returned and she was eventually able to cry and express feelings again. Psychotherapy groups, churches and other support can all help to battle soullessness.

Spirituality

Being part of a spiritual fellowship where people show love and community creates a sense of family and prepares the soil of our hearts for growth. Being loved helps people to repair and rejuvenate themselves.

Art

Art has a very powerful humanizing affect on our lives. Henri Nouwen, in his book *The Return of the Prodigal Son*, discusses Rembrandt's painting of the father receiving the prodigal son.[9] It is a beautiful work portraying the father lovingly opening his arms to receive his son in a gentle and tender way. Art can help us to open our souls to appreciate beauty.

Tragedy

We should never desire to prescribe tragedy, which is always painful, but there is no doubt that it sometimes opens our hearts for the first time. Strange as it may seem, sometimes during a terrible loss we are confronted with our repressed inner lives and the buds of our soul begin to grow, opening us to feel sadness and work through our grieving. We can then open to the love which we were previously unable to see. Some of the most soulful people I've met have experienced the most suffering.

Contemplative prayer

Exposing our souls to the naked influence of God's love has a way of opening our hearts, melting our false selves, and allowing us to open to love in our true selves in God. The love of God is able to melt away the false self and open us to the love of each other and ourselves. This is discussed further in later chapters.

JOHN'S STORY

John was drinking in a bar when the verdict of the O.J. Simpson trial was announced. He was extremely upset by the verdict, and became so angry that he literally broke up the bar. He was eventually referred to my office. John related his extreme anger at the verdict to the death of his wife, fifteen years ago, when she was executed on the job. The O.J. trial reminded him of his own experience of going through a lengthy trial process followed by a long road of hurt and disaster in his life. He became an alcoholic then a cocaine addict, and was unable to take care of his children. Without his wife he could not give them the support, nurture, and love they needed. As a result he felt as though his life was destroyed; he had become soulless. Angry and indifferent to people, he was destroying himself with alcohol and cocaine. He described how he would get his gun and shoot up his room. Working with him was scary and I wondered if he would become violent towards me in our sessions.

After working together for six months his heart settled and he seemed less angry. He started to attend a church in the local area and would always do the homework for our sessions—writing letters and doing exercises. As the therapy continued he became more balanced and alive within. Able to express himself, he grieved his wife's death and the pain he had caused his children by his destructive life. As time went on he talked increasingly about the concept of forgiveness. It appeared that the more work we did together, the more he was released from the hurt and anger in his heart and developed a sense of forgiveness.

Then one evening John went to see the film Dead Man Walking in which a nun is instrumental in seeking forgiveness for a murderer. At our next session I was surprised to hear him say that he wanted to go to the state where his wife's murderer was in prison, to forgive him. I was shocked and unconvinced that this was his real aim. John tried a number of avenues to be admitted to the prison but was blocked in every way, until eventually through contacts in a politician's office, he was enabled to go there. When he arrived he was introduced to the prisoner, who was in a glass bulletproof cage. Expressing his feelings, John told the prisoner how his wife's murder had destroyed his life, filled him with hatred, and made him destructive to himself and to his children. His life was all messed up. But then, he told the prisoner, he had come to realize through his work in therapy and his spiritual insights that unless he learnt to forgive he would further destroy himself. The hurt in his heart would make him even more bitter and destructive. With much pain and tears, John forgave his wife's murderer.

When John next came to see me he appeared relaxed and I was keen to find out what had happened. He said to me, "It was very difficult at first, but then it became very easy, because the prisoner reminded me of you, he looked just like you." The time we spent together in psychotherapy result-ed in a powerful connection growing between us. Seeing the prisoner, John projected our relationship on to the prisoner and was able to forgive him. Is it possible then, that forgiveness requires a prior relationship or experience of love in order for someone to let go of the hurt and anger that were caused? I don't know, but it seemed that our work together and the love that developed between us allowed John to open his heart in forgiveness. John has now stopped using cocaine, no longer drinks alcohol, and has moved out West. Recently he sent me a picture of his new bride, and described his life as very positive; free of the anger and hurt which were so destructive. In opening his heart to grieve the pain and hurt of the murder of his wife, along with his spiritual prayer life, he experienced a new sense of openness involving forgiveness and love, and was able to connect with himself, God, his children, and others. Is this not the movement from soullessness to soulfulness!

REFERENCES

1. Ivan Klima, *The Spirit of Prague and Other Essays*, trans. Paul Wilson (London: Granta, 1994).

2. Alfred Tennyson, *In Memorium: A.H.H* (1850).

3. Georgia O'Keefe, "About Myself" in *Georgia O'Keefe: One Hundred Flowers,* ed N. Calloway (New York: Random House, 1987).

4. Ivan Klima, *The Spirit of Prague and Other Essays,* trans. Paul Wilson (London: Granta, 1994).

5. Timothy McCartney, (personal communication).

6. Reinhold Niebuhr, *The Irony of American History,* (New York: Simon & Schuster, 1952).

7. Rollo May, *My Quest for Beauty* (Dallas: Saybrook, 1985), 242.

8. Herbert Read, *Art and Alienation: The Role of the Artist in Society* (New York: Viking, 1967), 21.

9. Henri J. M. Nouwen, *The Return of the Prodigal Son: A Story of Homecoming* (New York: Doubleday, 1992).

CHAPTER 3
ANGER: THE BRUTAL GIFT

Of the Seven Deadly Sins, anger is possibly the most fun. To lick your wounds, to smack your lips over grievances long past, to roll over your tongue the prospect of bitter confrontations still to come, to savor to the last toothsome morsel both the pain you are given and the pain you are giving back - in many ways it is a feast fit for a king. The chief drawback is that what you are wolfing down is yourself. The skeleton at the feast is you. (Frederick Buechner[1])

It sounds paradoxical to include anger in a discussion on contemplation, but contemplation is certainly impacted by anger. Anger is one of the most powerful emotions in our modern culture. Anger is a neutral feeling that can be used for constructive or positive action, as when anger at an injustice or evil drives us to try and remedy the situation. Jesus' anger in the temple is a clear example of this (Matthew 21:12-13). The problems occur when anger is allowed to linger as it blocks our ability to love.

Anger is a normal reaction to some circumstances, and there is nothing wrong with being angry. The key issue is how we manage the anger. The news media are filled with stories of road rage, air rage, and yacht rage; Columbine, numerous instances of children acting violently, violent video games and many other examples indicate to us that our modern culture is saturated with anger. Anger is the leading cause of intimacy dysfunction among couples, families, friends, churches, synagogues, political parties, and other social groupings.

By the age of forty-five or fifty, many of us confront shattered dreams and live with the painful reality of what might have been. We can choose to live the rest of our lives in a state of anger and frustration or we can recognize our failures and losses, learn to grieve the pain, and open ourselves to a lifestyle of faithfulness and gratitude. In order to understand the deeper parts of our hearts, to experience the love of our true selves in God, we must choose to deal with the angry feelings in our hearts. Otherwise they will contaminate every area of our lives, and impede contemplation. In contemplation we may experience the reformation of emotions so that anger, instead of being a threat, becomes a positive motivating force to fight injustice and other wrongs of the world.

In my work as a consulting psychiatrist, I have been struck over the past five to ten years by the number of people of all ages coming to me with issues associated with anger. Anger takes many forms. It may present as a disgruntled or complaining attitude, violent activity, a grudge against a family member, hatred towards another person or towards oneself, intimacy dysfunction, depression, or a painful experience of betrayal. Prevalent in modern culture, anger disrupts our relationships making it difficult to open to a deeper form of spirituality (contemplation) that would enable us to move from our false, defensive selves to our true selves in God. Contemplation requires a willingness to face our deep hurts and deal with the anger that paralyzes our lives and our relationships.

CAUSES OF ANGER

Anger has many causes and it would be difficult to provide a comprehensive discussion in this short chapter. Anger is usually associated with hurt, which often has its origin in childhood. Children are fragile. Feeling pain, they find it difficult to process or grieve the pain. Much of the hurt and anger of our childhood trauma is repressed and does not present itself until we are provoked in our adult lives; adult anger is often a delayed reaction from childhood.

Deprivation of instinctual needs

A generally accepted theory of child development is that a child has three basic instinctual needs. Firstly, survival and security; will I survive and if so how secure will I be? Secondly, affection and esteem; who will love me and how will I feel about myself? And thirdly, power and control; will I have some autonomy over my life? Life is wounded and all of us, particularly as children, have been hurt in one or all of these areas resulting in a powerful reaction of hurt and anger. Simultaneously, compensation occurs, making the instinctive need more intense, more pronounced and an end in itself.

Children hurt in the survival-security area feel a deep sense of abandonment—producing anger and a deep craving for more security that they may look for in people or possessions. Those hurt in affection-esteem suffer feelings of rejection—making them feel angry and motivated to find solace in various behaviors that include pleasing others and taking drugs. Those hurt in the power-control area have deep shame or humiliation issues—resulting in anger that energizes them to seek power through control and perfectionism. The deprivation of these instinctual needs is associated with deep hurt and anger in childhood and can continue throughout the rest of life.

The brain deals with this deprivation by developing a false mind-made self, which produces illusory emotional programs for happiness involving money (security), power, control, or pleasure. Anger then results both from the deprivation of our basic instinctual needs—survival/security, affection/esteem, and power/control—and also from any interference with whatever is being used to compensate for this deprivation. George was abandoned by his father, when he was a child. As an adult he found security in collecting books. He was angry about being abandoned, but also very angry if it was even suggested that he stop collecting books, although this behavior deprived his family of all their savings.

Fatigue and stress

Anger is commonly associated with fatigue and stress. Urgent time pressures, long hours of work, the burdens of family life, and the burgeoning information revolution whereby our office accompanies us everywhere, leave us fatigued, stressed, and angry. Others have written substantially on this issue, and I would particularly recommend Sigmund Freud's *Civilization and its Discontents*[2] and *Gift From The Sea* by Ann Morrow Lindbergh.[3]

Illness

Anger is associated with certain illnesses—psychiatric, neurological, and physical. Depression can be understood as anger acting toward the self (repressed rage) and anger as depression expressed outwardly. Anger can also be associated with bipolar disorder and some types of epilepsy. The physical conditions of diabetes and hypertension may also have anger associated with them. Traumatic injuries, especially head injuries, may result in anger. Anger clearly has a range of possible causational factors, which must all be considered when assessing its origin and manifestation.

Loss

Throughout our lives, one of the most common causes of anger is loss. All life involves change, all change involves loss, and all loss involves pain. Loss is ubiquitous. We lose everything in life: our age, our youth, our hair, our body parts, our jobs, and ultimately our lives. Loss, then, is a constant in life and always evokes a powerful grieving process. The grieving process has two major components—the anger pole and the grief pole. When we lose something or somebody we love, we are both angry and sad about the loss. In our culture many of us get stuck at the anger pole when we experience a loss. The anger pole makes us feel empowered and self-assertive, giving us an illusion of power but at the same time blocking our ability to open ourselves to the love around us. So we become isolated and disconnected from community.

On the other hand, at the grief pole we experience deep feelings of sadness and loss and sometimes even a sense of impotency. But grieving is healing—it empties our hearts and opens us to love and gratitude. Jesus said, "Blessed are those who mourn for they will be comforted" (Matthew 5:4). We have all been hurt in childhood and in a deep sense have a lot of crying to do. The next time we become angry it may be helpful to see if we can move from the anger pole to the grief pole and accept the grieving or sadness in our heart. Here lies the gift of liberation, freedom, and hope.

Facing the hurt and anger in our hearts is a vital process in the journey towards contemplation. God, in his grace, often enables us to face our hurt and anger and open ourselves to him, despite our inability to address these issues on our own. Contemplative prayer involves unloading the unconscious, which loosens the bonds of our repressed hurt and anger, allowing us to become authentic. All hurt is synergistic and has a post-traumatic effect; as we articulate and work through our hurt so we are liberated from it. Psychotherapy and contemplation both deal with the emptying, or the clearing, of the heart—the unloading of the unconscious. In psychotherapy we talk or give words or images to release our pain, but in the silence and stillness of contemplation the body unloads its pain in other ways, maybe with grunts, twitches, or coughs.

Although controversial, exploring the unconscious life of our dreams can be important because many times we are unable to face the painful issues of our life in a purely conscious state. We need to recognize that often our dreams are trying to share with us the deeper side of our hearts, or our true selves. God, the lover or dreamer, often reaches out to us, the beloved, in our dreams. A simple prayer before sleep asks God to clear our hearts or psyches to allow him to come to us. Recording our dreams in a diary helps us to see what God is doing in us. Please note that only God the Dreamer knows the dream. It is a gift; so let us accept it in love with a willingness to learn.

DYNAMICS OF ANGER

Anger can be understood as a post-traumatic effect resulting from the repressed anger of childhood and is built upon by hurtful experiences in later life. In other words, much of the anger we feel today results from the hurt we experienced yesterday or in our early childhood. There are a few important issues, which may help us to clarify and understand the process of anger in our lives. First of all, when we become angry our bodies experience a powerful physiological change called the Diffuse Physiological Arousal (DPA), in which blood pressure and pulse rise and our bodies prepare for the fight or flight reaction.

Males, when aroused, have a much more difficult time self-soothing or calming down than females. In fact males tend to settle down best after they have sought revenge. All this wear and tear from the anger response and the inability to self-soothe takes its toll and may help to explain why men die younger than women.

When we become extremely angry we stop using our higher brain-power, and behave much more instinctively. Unable to benefit from the use of our cortex, we find it difficult to learn from previous experiences or to use our rational faculties effectively. As we become angrier we become less human in behavior, acting without wisdom or guidance. In such a state we can be dangerous to ourselves or others. As DPA occurs and our pulse rises about 10 per cent above normal, our intelligence drops, leaving us retarded and irrational. In a 2002 seminar at Harvard Medical School on how to cope with very difficult children, the professor described that we have to connect with the child before the anger becomes so intense that the IQ drops significantly. He said it is possible to still work with a child who has lost five to ten IQ points, but as the anger rises and IQ drops by 30 points it is almost impossible to communicate. At this point the angry person is in a state of functional retardation and unable to discuss things from a rational perspective. In my experience you cannot really talk to a very, very angry person. The time to talk things over is after their anger has subsided.

In a heated discussion, when the other person's anger is increasing, we can help them by listening empathically and taking a calm approach. Yet because of our co-dependency and desire to please, we persist in trying to reason with the angry person even though it's a waste of time, leading to useless argument and sometimes to destructive behavior. This explains why some people, particularly men, become extremely violent when they are angry. Take the example of a man who becomes very angry, his pulse and blood pressure rise and he and looses much of his reasoning power. He is already acting in a subnormal or retarded state, and then he goes to a liquor store or bar and has a drink. Reduced reasoning powers combined with decreased inhibitions from alcohol are an explosive mix. This may explain why so much violence is domestic. The Commissioner of Police of the Bahamas has said that in the past three years 50 per cent of all murders were related to domestic or relationship violence. Sadly, the person who we love the most often makes us the most angry. As one person said, "I've never thought of divorce, but I must say I have thought of murder!"

Anger causes us to lose a sense of the present. Attached to the hurts of the past, our minds are caught in a past-future prison. This occurs because the hurts of the past can project painful images onto the screen of the future, making us ignore or avoid the present. A problem may be quite easy to resolve, but while we are angry we are divorced from the present and caught up in a past-future prison, and so we miss the opportunity to do this.

Anger is often the root cause of intimacy dysfunction, causing the breakdown of committed couples, families, friendships, and communities. As anger becomes more widespread in modern culture, we find it increasingly difficult to experience intimacy and grow in relationships. The spiritual journey is, at its heart, an antidote to destructive anger—allowing us to open ourselves in love to our true selves in God. Scripture warns us not to sin when we are angry and not to let the sun set on our anger, so that roots of bitterness will not poison our relationships (Ephesians 4:26,27).

STAGES OF ANGER

It is useful to talk about stages of anger, but these do not necessarily occur in a clear-cut, sequential pattern and should only be used as a framework to help us think about the difficult issues. These three stages of anger are hypothetical and do not provide a comprehensive perspective but, influenced by my own experience and work, offer an outline to help us appreciate the power and destructiveness of the anger process.

Hurt

The first stage of anger is always hurt, which occurs primarily in childhood. Children are very sensitive to hurt, which is often completely unintentional. For example, a child is sucking at its mother's breast; the telephone rings and the mother leaps up, the breast slipping from the child's mouth. For the mother the interruption is unimportant—the phone needs answering; but for the child it registers as an experience of rejection or abandonment. Children are extremely vulnerable to pain because they are unable to process or grieve it and as a result they repress it to be expressed in later life.

Anger

In the second stage hurt becomes anger. As anger increases, it may move into a strong affective response known as rage. Rage is often the reaction to a shaming or humiliating event. In rage there is a powerful diffuse physiological arousal and, generally speaking, a person is unable to think clearly and can become violent. As time goes on, if the anger is not addressed, it moves into our hearts or psyches and becomes resentment. Resentment comes form two Latin words, *re* (again) and *sentir* (to feel). When the anger goes into our hearts and becomes resentment, it means we feel it again and again. The anger becomes like a vacuum cleaner, scooping up all the hurts of our life, creating a major bolus of pain.

Resentment has a powerful effect on our lives. In fact, when we resent someone we give them power to control us. We give them our authority card—our meaning, dignity, identity, and value. We take them on vacation with us. We take them to bed with us. We spend every waking hour thinking of them. Resentment hurts the heart and gives away our control to another person or situation. Another dynamic not generally recognized is that resentment becomes embedded in our hearts, we become addicted to it and it dictates our lives.

This resentment then produces roots of bitterness, which extend into all aspects of our lives, possibly affecting our physical bodies in the form of headaches, low back pain, and other illnesses like depression. It also influences our close relationships and sometimes our dealings with strangers. Bitterness gives life a sour taste, and all events, regardless how positive, are seen from a negative perspective. It may be a beautiful day, but for the bitter person it is too hot; it may be a lovely party, but the bitter person complains that the music is too loud. The bitter person sees negativity in every part of life, and because life is wounded they usually find it. A bitter person can brighten up a room just by leaving it.
Many young people, because of the hurt they have experienced—the loss of the nuclear family, extended family, and community—experience deep hurt in their hearts and roots of bitterness spring up. What a difference to visit one person in a nursing home who is grateful, working through their anger and hurt, and who still has a positive view of life as opposed to another person who has closed their heart, become hard-hearted, angry,

and bitter. Their physical circumstances may be similar, but their experiences and outlooks are very different.

Grudge

If anger is not addressed it moves on to form a grudge. A grudge is a bitter feeling that becomes embedded in a person's heart and usually occurs between two people who were once close to each other and had a painful falling out. The grudge means there is a permanent hatred, separation, and isolation. Grudges occur between husbands and wives, children and parents, females and males, different races, and different nationalities. Grudges may be trans-generational, passed down from grandparents to parents to children.

A classic example of a grudge is found in the story of John the Baptist (Mark 6:21-28). Salome, the daughter of Herodias, danced so beautifully at King Herod's birthday party that he promised her a gift—anything up to half of his kingdom. With such an offer, this dear young lady could have had whatever she wanted—a castle on the Mediterranean or all her college bills paid. But instead she went home to her mother Herodias to ask her advice. Herodias had a grudge against John the Baptist because he spoke out against her affair with King Herod. She had caused John to be imprisoned in a dungeon, but she still wasn't satisfied. Acting on her grudge, Herodias told Salome to ask King Herod for the head of John the Baptist on a plate. Against his will, but bound by his promise, King Herod had John the Baptist beheaded and his head brought to Herodias on a plate.

It was not an axe that killed John the Baptist, it was a grudge. Grudges kill the life of our hearts, destroy our families, poison our communities, and create intimacy dysfunction. But most sadly they destroy the possibility of a deeper sense of contemplation and interrupt the mission of God's love in the world. If we seek to move to a deeper spirituality and open to the concept of contemplation, we have to deal with the grudges in our lives.

Grudges result from the hardness of our hearts. This may be described best by Jesus' parable of the sower. In the story Jesus said that while the farmer was sowing seed, some of the seed fell on stony ground, failed to grow, and the birds ate it. This illustrates that the seeds of love cannot penetrate our hardened hearts and the forces of evil, represented in the story by the birds, neutralize the love that does exist. Long-term unaddressed anger hardens our hearts making them fertile ground for evil. Evil destroys the meaningful quality of life leading to the creation of darkness, despair, disharmony, and most sadly the destruction of hope.

I have witnessed this phenomenon in deeply hurt young men and women addicted to cocaine who described to me how, at certain points in their lives, they were very aware of the force of good on one hand and the force of evil on the other. They were freely accepting responsibility for the choices that were theirs and theirs alone. One addict, who had killed three times, said he was aware of two conflicting forces—one for good and one for evil, and to kill he would always choose the force for evil. He went on to tell me that one day while his mother was visiting him in prison, she said that she had been praying he would choose the force for good. Shocked by this, to his surprise he found himself praying to God for forgiveness and mercy. Since then he has been seeking the force for good.

MALADAPTIVE EXPRESSIONS OF ANGER

We all have anger and express it in some form or another, but many of us have maladaptive and destructive ways of expressing anger. Following are a few styles; you may be able to add others!

The bomb

This person is very pleasant and kind at work. They have a long fuse, but when they do explode it usually occurs at home, frightening the spouse and terrifying the children. After the explosion they feel much better and may even want to throw a party. After one such explosion, a man could not understand why his children and wife did not want to enjoy the pizza he had bought for them, he had forgotten his explosion. But in truth they were walking on eggshells, terrified that he would explode again. This has a terrible effect on children because they tend to be egocentric and blame themselves for the parent's behavior.

The scorekeeper

This person does not react immediately when they are hurt or angry but keeps score. When they do burst out, they bring up issues that happened today, yesterday, last week, last year, and maybe even ten years ago. Even though we may try to reach a rational understanding with them, angry outbursts continue. One lady brought me a little black book in which her husband detailed everything she had done wrong over the past three years. With the pain of realizing that she was in a relationship with someone who was putting a magnifying glass on every mistake she made by recording it, she went into a nervous collapse.

The velvet harpoon champion

This person appears very pleasant on the surface, but meeting them at the church Christmas party, well dressed and smiling they ask: "Have you gained a few pounds?" If you react, they retort, "Oh, did I make you angry?" Their words appear innocent and velvet-like, but they know how to pierce our hearts with their harpoons. Often we do not feel the hurt immediately. Later, lying in bed at home, we wonder, "How could they say or do that to me?" When we see them next their lovely smile disarms us, and we find ourselves vulnerable again to their barbs. Finally we get the message, and when we see them coming we protect ourselves by moving away.

The deep-freeze

This person becomes quiet, distant, and cold when angry. A pilot shared that when his wife makes him angry he doesn't speak to her for two weeks. At the end of two weeks he claims she is pliable and submissive. This terrible, destructive stonewalling is more common in men, but is also used by women. The end result is hurt, resentment, and intimacy dysfunction.

The gang fighter

This person is unable to express anger alone and feels empowered to express their anger when surrounded by certain friends. They do it either by not acknowledging us although they know us well, or by some destructive or negative act which is extremely painful.

The guerrilla fighter

This person expresses anger in a passive-aggressive way rather than openly. They may talk about us behind our backs. Gossiping is a form of guerrilla fighting, and is very destructive to relationships.

The persistent complainer

This person is always complaining all the time, no matter what has happened. They are never grateful and can find a negative side to everything. They learned long ago that by expecting nothing they would never be disappointed!

The button pusher

This person convinces us of their confidence and loyalty, they encourage us to share our heart-felt secrets with them, promising things will go no further. To our dismay, when they are not with us, they have no difficulty betraying us by sharing our secrets. Deeply painful, such hurts may continue for a lifetime.

In addition many of us use drugs, alcohol, and various forms of psychological defense, like blaming others, to express anger. All these are always maladaptive and destroy intimacy in our personal and interpersonal lives. Through God's grace we can move beyond these.

ANGER AND CONTEMPLATION

As we open our lives to a deeper experience of God in contemplation it is important to hear the words of David,

> Search me, O God and know my heart; test me and know my anxious thoughts. See if there is any offensive way in me, and lead me in the way everlasting (Psalm 139:23,24).

Journeying toward authenticity or contemplation requires total commitment—to be brutally honest in dealing with our anger and facing those hurt parts of our hearts we have not processed. In other words, by the grace of God we have to break up the unplowed ground of our hearts, which harbors hurts or resentments that took place years ago. As David says, "O Lord…give me an undivided heart, that I may fear your name" (Psalm 86:11). In life our hearts are spread through so many different places; work, home, family, friends, pain, joy. This leaves us fragmented. Coming home from work, my mother would say, "Let me catch myself." I always wondered what she meant. Now I think I understand. During the pressures of the day, our hearts become spread thin between our many activities and concerns. Coming home at night and sitting quietly to catch or recollect herself my mother took time to still her heart. Then she was truly able to open in love to her children and those around her. To repeat David's words, "Give me an undivided heart, that I may fear your name" (Psalm 86:11).

Anger is a brutal gift of love, inviting us to face ourselves: a message from our hearts to come home. Anger is one of the commonest pathways to deep contemplation because, by facing our anger and dealing with it, we make the authentic journey home to our hearts. By working through our feelings of abandonment, rejection, and shame we can move to a deeper level, beyond our defensive false selves to open to our true selves in God. Anger is a map telling us where we have been and predicting where we will end up. Making the inner journey to face our hearts leads to true contemplation because, when we go to the deepest parts of our hearts, we are never alone but enter the presence of God who is the foundation and fulfillment of our beings. The deeper we go into our hearts to face ourselves, in a mysterious but beautiful way we open to God—the one from whom we came, the one whose love will never let us go and whose face will never turn away.

ANGER MANAGEMENT

In the journey of contemplation, seeking intimacy in a distant world, we will experience hurt and anger. Therefore, we need to be focused and willing to deal with our anger. I have found these nine steps are often helpful to people.

1. Keep an anger diary.

No matter how slight the incident, write it up and look at what causes it, how it is expressed, and if there is any connection to your early child-hood experiences. Writing requires us to think things through, conceptualize them, put them on paper and they in turn speak back to us. It is a powerful way of helping us to understand the inner workings of our hearts and our lives. An anger diary clears our hearts of anger, opening us to a deeper form of love—the love of God.

2. Know what makes me angry.

Different circumstances make different people angry. Some of us have been hurt through criticism, disappointment, rejection, abandonment, or shame, but we have all been hurt in some way. It is very important to know what makes us angry.

3. Know how I get angry.

We all have individual ways of behaving when angry; some of us become tense, others become quiet, some are noisy, others go red, and some may shake. If we know what makes us angry and how we behave when angry, we are better prepared to deal with anger.

4. Take timeout.

When we are angry it is important to recognize the fact and take time-out to self-soothe. Self-soothing occurs in contemplative prayer where we quiet ourselves, focus our intention on God and consent to his presence and the action of his unconditional love in our lives. This is a calming experience that renews our perspective. Women self-soothe more quickly than men. Men are sometimes unable to self-soothe until they have sought revenge. But revenge can have serious consequences. Some of us seek to self-soothe by taking a drink, but this creates havoc because as the anger increases, our ability to reason decreases, and drinking alcohol destroys our inhibitions creating a walking time bomb.

5. Use an anger prayer.

Anger can be so overwhelming that we forget we are people loved by God; the anger is just a feeling, not our defining character. A simple prayer like "Lord God have mercy on me" can remind us. This concept of transcendence—that God loves us and made us in his own image—anchors us in our God-given personhood, and prayer allows us to face and deal appropriately with the angry feelings. When our kids become angry they can destroy themselves through suicide or destroy others through homicide. Prayer or timeout really allows us to settle.

6. Process my anger.

When we see how anger connects to hurts over our recent past and early childhood, we realize that life is not a disconnected group of events; all the events of our lives are connected from the womb to the day we die. Thus processing our anger can reveal many hidden life-changing insights.

7. Discuss the situation.

After completing the pervious six steps it may be helpful to discuss the situation with the persons involved. Discussing the situation without working the previous steps may be inflammatory, creating further distance. Sometimes the others involved are unwilling to discuss the situation. This need not prevent us from reaching closure.

8. Confess my anger.

Anger is such a painful emotion and the hurt so deep that we have to give up, or confess, the anger to a friend, a therapist, a priest, or directly to God. Prayer, particularly contemplative prayer, allows us to give up our anger and hurt and open ourselves in quietness before God. As this occurs there is an unloading of unconscious pain or hurt, which may be manifested as twitching behavior, coughs, or various somatic pains. As the body releases its hurt and anger, it becomes still.

9. Seek forgiveness.

The topic of forgiveness is an enormous one, about which much has been written. Suffice it to say here that forgiveness is not some mystical process. It is a very personal process, where we deal with the hurt and anger in our hearts and prevent it from contaminating our lives by allowing us to open in love to true contemplation. Anger always requires forgiveness, and this involves working through, or letting go of, the pain attached to the incidents of our lives. Being forgiven does not mean that we forget, but when these incidents return to consciousness they no longer have the power to hurt, but are empty shells.

HEALING THE CHILD WITHIN

After I gave a talk on anger in Italy, Maria approached me to say that she was very angry. I asked about her life and she told me that when she was six years old her mother died of cancer. It was a very painful time, but she had little memory of the circumstances around her mother's death. She recalled, however, that her mother asked her to go and live with a friend who also had a little girl. She remembered this as being a very painful experience because she felt that the woman tended to favor her own daughter and would treat Maria unfairly. As a result, Maria left her mother's friend and returned to live with her father and grandmother.

I asked Maria to tell me more of what she remembered about her mother's death. She did remember standing outside a church with a crucifix. She remembered stopping, feeling very sorry, and crying for Jesus. Obviously, she felt sorry for Jesus but she was also crying for herself. I then asked Maria if she would spend the next evening writing a letter to her mother at the time she was dying. At first she rebelled and said she couldn't do it. But the next day she brought a few lines and cried profusely. She said that as she sat down to write, she felt blocked—the pain in her heart was so heavy that she just cried and cried. The few lines she wrote went something like this: "Dear Mom, I am sorry you died. I wish you could have gotten better and been my friend to help me in life." then she just stopped and cried profusely.

Asking her if she could recall more about her mother, she said that her mother was in hospital for some reason but when things became worse she moved home to die. I asked Maria to write a letter to herself, the little girl age six, at the time of her mother's death. Again she found this very difficult and started to cry and said she couldn't do it. I begged her to please try. The next day she brought a short letter and started to tell me what happened. She had started to write the letter, but found it very difficult. She was able to write a few lines by imagining that she was high on the balcony of an eight-story building looking down on a little girl age six sitting in the garden below. The letter went something like this: "Dear little one, I am sorry that your mother died. It is very sad and life will be hard for you but you must try your best." The paper was stained with tears and reading it she cried profusely. Despite her tears, Maria felt it was quite impossible to get in touch with the pain of what had happened.

The next day I lectured again, and talked about how, by getting in touch with our pain through the appropriate grief mechanisms, we can empty our hearts of pain and open them to love, gratitude, and a new enthusiasm for life. At the end of the lecture a little six-year-old girl I knew called Pricilla ran to me. I found myself walking towards Maria with Pricilla in my arms. When Maria saw me with the little girl she made the connection between Pricilla and her own six-year-old self, and ran from the building screaming. Pricilla's dad came up and, sensing what was going on, was very supportive. After a while, Maria ventured back into the building and approached us. Like a frightened child she would touch Pricilla's arm and then quickly withdraw. Finally she hugged Pricilla and started crying. She cried and cried. It was touching to see the healing bond between Maria and Pricilla.

The next day Maria explained that when she saw little Pricilla, she was able to get in touch with the memory of herself as a little girl for the first time. She saw how vulnerable she was, how difficult it must have been to lose her mother at such a tender age. Now she understood why she didn't remember—the memories were too painful and had been repressed. But she said something interesting happened after she cried. She found herself being freer, feeling lighter, less bitter, and less angry as her heart emptied of grief and hurt.

A few months later I received a letter from one of Maria's friends telling me that Maria's life was now very different. The week we worked together had a powerful effect on her and, when she returned to Sicily, she made a point of visiting people she had hurt to apologized to them. This is no quick fix, because she will have to continue to work through the issues of the hurt in her heart for the rest of her life, but her life has changed, she is now less angry, more peaceful, and is having a meaningful impact on her local community.

COPING WHEN OTHERS ARE ANGRY WITH YOU

Perhaps the most difficult problem is coping when other people are angry with us. Many of us have been wounded by persons who were angry with us or at least that we perceived to be angry with us. What I call the Abigail response is relevant, simple, and effective in dealing with these situations.

Abigail was an attractive, intelligent woman who was married to an obnoxious, cantankerous, alcoholic man named Nabal. He was extremely rich and very proud of his accomplishments. Meanwhile, David was in hiding from the jealous rage of King Saul (1Samuel 24,25). Hungry, tired, and frustrated, David asked his men to go to Nabal's farm and ask for food and water. This was a reasonable request, especially since David's men had protected Nabal's sheep from thieves. Nabal was enraged: "Why should I take my bread and water, and the meat I have slaughtered for my shearers, and give it to men coming from who knows where?" (1Samuel 25:11).

The men returned, telling David of Nabal's response. Recognizing the desperate state of his men, David became viciously angry with Nabal. He organized four hundred men into an army and set off to destroy Nabal, his family, and his estate. David's men were drifters, dropouts, and vagabonds. In modern terms they were burnt out drug addicts, criminals, and alcoholics. These were men who could not make it in the government forces of King Saul. Tired, hungry, and frustrated, they had little self-control and were unpredictable, making them even more vicious and destructive.

One of Nabal's workers saw David and his army approaching. Petrified, he ran to Nabal's wife Abigail to tell her. Explaining the situation, he shared how David had sent his men to request food and water from Nabal, but were refused. The worker explained that David's men had been very kind to them in helping to protect the sheep. He apologized for coming directly to Abigail but said that he had no choice because Nabal would lose his temper and not deal with the situation.

CONFLICT RESOLUTION

Abigail's response illustrates ten principles, which will help us to cope when other people are angry with us.

1. Develop a sense of identity

The most effective characteristic in dealing with an angry person is having a sense of one's own identity—a sense of being somebody. People without a sense of identity are seriously threatened by people who are angry with them. The anger towards them is perceived as a threat, as being unloved. As a result they feel guilty, ashamed, and will do anything to please or conform. This is a particular characteristic of codependents who have their identities outside of themselves and spend their lives trying to please or conform. Abigail, though living at a time and in a part of the world where a woman had less rights than men, had a sense of herself. Her husband's staff knew she could be depended upon to deal effectively with difficult situations. A sense of identity involves a unity of personality with a core of unchanging stability, allowing a person to be proactive and creative in times of crisis. However, with the breakdown of the family and the fragmentation of society as a whole, maintaining a secure identity in our times may be difficult. In this ever-changing world people need an unchanging core. Faith in God—who remains the same yesterday, today, and forever—provides an unchanging core in changing times. Abigail had faith and a clear sense of identity. Therefore she was proactive; she was responsible and dependable and based her decisions on values rather than feelings or circumstances.

2. Recognize the problem

Abigail immediately sensed the gravity of the situation. There was no time for denial, such as "This can't happen to me," or "The worker is exaggerating." She didn't use projection or blaming "It's Nabal's fault," or "Nabal created this mess, he'd better get us out of it." She didn't use magical thinking "Everything will work out OK," or "David is a godly man, he won't hurt us." She didn't use religious sentimentally "Don't worry, God will handle it." or "We're Christians, God won't let anything happen to us."

No, Abigail broke through all those defenses and recognized that if she did not act, she and her family would be destroyed.

3. Act immediately

Recognizing the seriousness of the situation, Abigail moved immediately into action. Having a clear sense of herself and being proactive, she did not react or panic, but responded immediately and effectively. Abigail ordered her workers to prepare donkeys laden with food. The food included two hundred loaves of bread, two jugs of wine, five sheep, grain, raisins, and two hundred cakes. Organizing the food on donkeys, she sent them ahead and followed behind on her own beast.

4. Listen empathetically

Meeting David and his men as they came down the mountain to Nabal's estate, Abigail and her men listened as David spewed out his anger and venom about her husband. A very important principle, empathic listening is a way of allowing the angry person to vent and express their feelings. It involves listening objectively. It means listening the angry person into being—so they can empty themselves of their powerful angry feelings. An angry person is so full of their feelings that it is a waste of time to explain, or talk to them while they are very angry. Once they have expressed their anger it is more feasible for them to hear what you have to say. It requires restraint and patience to let the angry person express their anger. Of course this requires a sense of security in oneself to be able to stand there patiently and be shouted at. There can be no understanding of another without listening to them. A parent once said, "I can't understand my son because he never listens to me." If he really wants to understand his son, he has to spend time listening to him. Abigail did just that. She stayed there quietly listening to David venting his anger.

5. Show respect

An angry person is essentially hurt. So following the hurt trail may enable one to cope more effectively with the anger. Being hurt, the person's self-esteem is threatened, they feel undervalued and without respect.

Therefore, showing the angry person genuine respect will go a long way towards helping them feel better about themselves. Abigail, after listening to David, dismounted her donkey, bowed down to the ground and called him, "My Lord." This too is not easy when someone is angry with you. But showing meekness and respect helps to soothe the hurt. It also allows more effective healing of the hurt after the anger is expressed. In modern life we have become careless about manners and decent behavior. Saying "thank you," "please," and "you're welcome," enhances the development of positive attitudes in others and ourselves.

6. Admit responsibility

Although Abigail was not the one who rejected David's request, as Nabal's wife she admitted her share of the responsibility for what occurred. So often we put all the blame on others and are unwilling to take our share of the responsibility. Admitting responsibility allows the angry person to curtail his anger, and facilitates the mediation and resolution of the problem. But it takes a clear sense of self and identity to be secure enough to take responsibility and admit wrongdoing.

7. Be honest

Abigail admits to David that her husband is a difficult man because of his temper and alcohol problem. She recognizes the hurt and rejection meted out to David and his men by her husband's selfishness. Honesty, like taking responsibility, allows the situation causing the hurt and anger to be brought out into the open. Then the anger can be expressed more freely and the problems resolved more easily.

8. Be kind

Recognizing the abject state of frustration of David and his men, Abigail gives them a special gift of food and drink. Simple as it sounds, kindness goes a long way. The appropriate gift given at the right time can have a powerful healing effect on a person who is distraught or angry. "A gift given in secret soothes anger" (Proverbs 21:14).

9. Seek forgiveness

After giving David the gift, Abigail asks his forgiveness. In doing so she recognizes the importance of transcendence. Expressing her faith in the higher power of God, she says to David "As the Lord lives, forgive me." As discussed earlier, forgiveness—the process of giving up the hurt and roots of the anger—requires a greater perspective than the normal human one of stimulus and response. It is hard to give up a hurt that has riveted to your soul. However, the realization that God forgives us—puts aside the many times we fail him—lays the basis for us forgiving each other. Appealing to the grace and love of the Lord, Abigail asks David to forgive her as God has forgiven him. To ask forgiveness is the quintessence of admitting wrongdoing and sincerely desiring to change. We may not feel that it was appropriate for Abigail to ask for forgiveness in this situation, but in times of serious conflict healing may only be possible when we ask for forgiveness for our part in the conflict—even if it is only 10 per cent and the other party's is 90 per cent. This takes courage.

10. Affirm others

Abigail tells David that he is fighting the battle of God and that he will be king someday. But she tells him humbly that when he is king he would not want it on his conscience that he destroyed a whole family of innocent people. Thus she affirms the goodness of David's cause and the eventual success of his battles. She appeals to his sense of justice and the kind of king he would like to be. Angry people are hurting and in need of affirmation. By affirming David, Abigail heals the wound and resolves the crisis. David is extremely impressed. In fact he extols her discernment and virtually thanks her for saving him from vengeance.

CONCLUSION

Anger is a powerful emotion, which wreaks havoc in the lives of individuals, families, churches, and nations. It is really difficult to deal with anger without a transcendent vision of the meaning of God's love in society. Such a vision offers an effective basis for forgiveness—forgiving others as God in Christ has forgiven you (Ephesians 4:32).

REFERENCES

1. Frederick Buechner, *Wishful Thinking: A Seeker's ABC* (San Francisco: San Francisco Harper, 1993), 2.

2. Sigmund Freud, *Civilization and its Discontents* (New York: WWW Norton and Inc., 1961).

3. Ann Morrow Lindbergh, *Gift From The Sea* (New York: Pantheon Books, 1983).

CHAPTER 4
THE FALSE SELF: THE INTERNAL SABOTEUR

It is the nature of the false self to save us from knowing the truth about our real selves, from penetrating the deeper causes of our unhappiness, from seeing ourselves as we really are—vulnerable, afraid, terrified, and unable to let our real selves emerge. (James Masterson[1])

If anyone would come after me, he must deny himself and take up his cross and follow me. (Mark 8:34)

Contemplation involves an appreciation of the vision of God, followed by the sincere commitment to serve the mission of God's love in the world. To have the vision without the mission is an empty experience, producing a sense of frustration and misguidance, while the mission of love without the vision of God in the world produces busyness and burnout. It is so easy to rush around with deep religious fervor exhausting ourselves and achieving nothing meaningful. Contemplation requires an understanding of the *false self* and the *true self.* The false self is created early in childhood as a protection against the pain of abandonment, rejection, and humiliation. This is appropriate and necessary for childhood. When we become adults and are able to think about these things, we need to work through our defensive, false selves so that they do not become the functional adult selves. Our false selves create an incessant flow of defenses, distorting our true selves (which are defined by God's love) and destroying our ability to be intimate with each other and ourselves. If we drop the trappings of the false self and open to love in the true self, we will experience a deep sense of freedom, joy, and peace.

Brennan Manning describes in a most poignant way the development of his false self:

> When I was eight, the imposter, or false self, was born as a defense against pain. The imposter within whispered, "Brennan, don't ever be your real self anymore because nobody likes you as you are. Invent a new self that everybody will admire and nobody will know." So I became a good boy—polite, well mannered, unobtrusive, and deferential. I studied hard, scored excellent grades, won a scholarship in high school and was stalked every waking moment by the terror of abandonment and a sense that nobody was there for me.
>
> I learned that perfect performance brought the recognition and approval I desperately sought. I orbited into an unfeeling zone to keep fear and shame at a safe distance. As my therapist remarked, "All these years there has been a steal trapdoor covering your emotions and denying you access to them." Meanwhile, the imposter I presented for public inspection was nonchalant and carefree.[2]

Moving from the clutches of our false selves to our true selves is only possible when we feel safe to be who we really are—loved and accepted by God. We have to live in the present moment and not escape into the past or project into the future. No one, and I repeat, no one gives up or reduces their false self unless they feel loved. In the story of the Velveteen Rabbit, replying to the rabbit's question of how can he become real, the skin horse says, "You need to find someone who loves you and then you become real." So too in our lives, only as we open ourselves to be loved by God and by the community around us can we in any way begin to drop the trappings of our false selves. God's love will never fail us.

Discovering the true self is the journey of opening ourselves to God's love. Equally, opening to God's love is a journey to our true selves. It is a journey from darkness into light. Quoting the Apostle Paul:

> For it is shameful even to mention what the disobedient do in secret. But everything exposed by the light becomes visible, for it is light that makes everything visible (Ephesians 5:12-14).

This is comforting because regardless of the state of our lives or how much we think we have fallen, when we are exposed to the light of God's love, situations which are difficult or tragic can be openings into new experiences of being and love.

It is important to realize that as we open to our true selves in love, we begin to touch the woundedness of our hearts and, as a result, lose our defensiveness. For many of us this is terrifying—as children we learned to cover up our hurts through many different defense mechanisms, and these have continued into adult life. The danger is that instead of becoming authentic as we become older, we journey along the road becoming increasingly inauthentic. The false self, these onion-like layers around us, protects us from the pain of our woundedness, but as we open to our true selves we come to realize that it is our very woundedness, our inner pain, that is the source of the healing power of God's love in our life. In pain we can see our need for God afresh and receive him anew. In addition this woundedness gives us empathy for others, which can be used by God.

This is explained beautifully in Thornton Wilder's play, *The Angel That Troubled the Waters,* which is based on John 5:14. It depicts a pool that has great powers of healing for the first to enter whenever an angel stirs its waters. A physician comes periodically, hoping to be the first in line and longing to be healed of his melancholy. Finally he's first in line as the water moves. Just as he is ready to step into the water, an angel appears and blocks his way, telling him to draw back because this is not his time. Pleading for help in a broken voice, the physician is told by the angel that healing is not for him. Eventually the angel explains:

> Without your wounds where would your power be? It is your melancholy that makes your low voice tremble into the hearts of men and women. The very angels themselves cannot

persuade the wretched and hurting children on earth as can one human being broken on the wheels of living, love, and service. Only wounded soldiers can serve. Physician, draw back.[3]

In a similar vein, Rainer Maria Rilke, in *Letters to a Young Poet,* explained the efficacy of his own gift: "Do not believe that he who seeks to comfort you lives untroubled among the simple and quiet words that sometimes do you good. His life has much difficulty and sadness and remains far behind yours or he would not otherwise have been able to find these words."[4]

As I travel along my own spiritual journey I have learnt that only when I feel safe with God do I truly feel safe with myself. In other words, to really know God is to know oneself. As we look for a deeper understanding of ourselves, we move through the center of ourselves opening into the foundation of our being, that is God. Knowing God allows us, like the prodigal, to run to the caring compassionate father so beautifully depicted by Rembrandt's painting of the Prodigal Son. The father receives us, asking no questions, allowing us to trust ourselves to his care and to open ourselves to others. In Georges Bernanos' *Diary of a Country Priest,* he describes how since his ordination he struggled with doubt, fear, anxiety, and insecurity. The last entry in his diary reads:

It's all over now. The strange mistrust I had of myself, of my own being, has flown, I believe, forever. That conflict is done. I am reconciled to myself, to the poor, poor shell of me. How easy it is to hate oneself! True grace is in forgetting; yet if pride could die in us, the supreme grace would be to love oneself in all simplicity as one would love any member of the Body of Christ. Does it really matter? Grace is everywhere.[5]

ORIGIN OF THE FALSE SELF

Saint Bernard of Clairvaux, a mystic of the Cistercian order, first described the concept of the false self in the twelfth century. In the twentieth century Thomas Merton, Henry Nouwen, and others popularized it. The writings of Father Thomas Keating and Basil Pennington have brought it into further prominence. The concept of the false self provides a bridge between psychiatry and theology. James Masterson, a psychoanalyst, has written extensively about the false self, and his work has helped to develop a contemporary understanding of this concept and provide helpful insight into the nature of a person from a psychological perspective. This work, combined with the work of Keating, Pennington, Merton, and Nouwen, offers a helpful psychological and spiritual perspective on the false self. In this chapter I draw heavily on this work and on the insights I have gained from my own psychiatric practice.

The three basic instinctual needs of a newborn child were explained in chapter 3. First, the child has a need for survival and security: will I survive and how secure will I be? This question stays with us throughout our lives, either consciously or unconsciously. Second, the child has a major need for affection: who will love me? When someone is there for the child and shows them love or kindness, this is internalized, allowing them to have a sense of themselves, which gives rise to self-esteem—a major part of human existence from birth to death. Third, the child wants a sense of power or control over their life. Hence the childhood stress on *my* blanket, *my* bed, and *my* toy. This desire for autonomy continues in adult life, where sometimes we try to instill ownership in places where we do not possess it.

Life is wounded. Theologically this means we are all flawed. In Freudian terms we are in conflict between Eros, the life force, and Thanatos, the death force. As Carl Jung would say, we all have our shadow or dark side and often respond to our shadow in others. The Apostle Paul puts it this way: "For what I do is not the good I want to do; no, the evil I do not want to do—this I keep on doing" (Romans 7:19). The reality is that life is wounded and as a result all of us have been hurt in one or more areas of basic instinctual need. Those of us hurt in survival/security area tend to have abandonment issues. It is important to note that three As always stick together—wherever there is *Anger,* underneath it is *Anxiety* and at its core is a sense of *Abandonment.* Those hurt in affection/esteem area have rejection issues. Unless it is neutralized in later life by doing our grief work, this tendency to be attached to rejection contaminates many aspects of our lives.

For example a gentleman with severe rejection issues would perceive rejection in many ordinary, everyday interactions. This reinforced his sense of inadequacy and increased his self-absorption. Those hurt in the power/control area have humiliation or shame issues. Shame essentially means that we feel we *are* a mistake, as opposed to guilt, which implies that we *made* a mistake. Shame is particularly powerful in certain cultures and has a detrimental effect on the lives of many people who fail in some areas of their lives. The false self, through shame, would even encourage death (suicide) rather than face the pain of failure. The deprivation of these basic instinctual needs leads to a powerful hurt trail of abandonment, rejection, and humiliation or shame, associated with issues of hurt, guilt, and grief. This occurs to some extent in even the most loving of families.

Children feel pain but find it very hard to grieve or process the pain. As a result, much of the pain of childhood is repressed and often remains an undifferentiated general feeling of hurt or fear. This generalized fear is a powerful dynamic that pervades our lives. Whenever there is deprivation, the brain tries to compensate. When children face issues of trauma involving abandonment, rejection, or humiliation the brain develops, through many neural mechanisms, a false mind or false self to compensate for the deprivation of instinctual needs. Children can only cope with a critical amount of pain. When mothers repeatedly left their children for a period of time the children would express their hurt by crying, and then become depressed. After a while, when the mothers returned, the children became detached. Once detachment occurs the child loses the bond with its mother and is, in some sense, doomed to isolation and pain.[6]

In the case of abandonment, the false self makes hurt a center of motivation, so that the person will do anything to feel safe or protected. This may be achieved by getting more friends, more marbles, or feeling that we have more toys. Sadly this process continues in adult life, where abandonment issues are compensated for by the collection of possessions. This is not to say that having possessions is wrong in itself, but when they are a compensation for abandonment, then possessing material goods or other kinds of opportunities becomes an end in itself.

Where there is rejection, the false self encourages us to compensate by seeking pleasure in addiction, or becoming co-dependent in seeking to please people, or becoming self-absorbed. This process of course occurs subtly and eventually we may find that our whole life style is devoted to avoiding feelings of rejection. In humiliation or shame, the false self compensates by creating a sense of perfectionism or being very controlling. It may manifest itself in a marriage where a person seeks absolute power or control, in politics where they want to be the *kingpin,* or in the church where they seek intense domination and may even use political status to sanctify the expression of their anger.

The false self, created as a powerful defense against childhood trauma, tells us that who we are depends on what we possess, what we do, our reputation, or our ability to please people. The futility of such thinking is obvious—it implies that when we lose what we possess, we are valued less; when we do not feel the way we like to feel, we are worth less; when our reputation is destroyed, so are we; when we lose power, we are nothing. This leaves the self extremely fragile and so the false self becomes entrenched as we get older, to protect us from the painful feelings of abandonment, rejection, and humiliation. As a result the false self does not only block us from our true selves, but blocks us from opening to the one from whom we come—the love that will never let us go and the face that will never turn away. It is important to remind ourselves that in God "we live and move and have our being" (Acts 17:28).

When children feel lonely or abandoned, they may create imaginary playmates to lessen the pain. In therapy, Anna described how as a child she developed a scene in her imagination where she had her own private beach. She would walk along this beach each day and receive art lessons from a very kind, chubby, French lady who would paint with her and then compliment her paintings. Anna was able to describe in amazing detail and intricacy being with this imaginary art teacher. She commented that even today, in adult life, she feels comforted, loved, and supported when she thinks of being with the imaginary art teacher. However strange, this is acceptable and understandable in childhood. As we grow up and become able to think about our feelings, the false selves that protected us in childhood develop onion-like layers and become consolidated to represent our adult selves. Unless we work through our childhood trauma or pain, then these false selves lead us on the journey to inauthenticity.

Another way to look at this is that when a child is hurt and cannot really deal with their feelings and is not accepted by the adults around them, the child buries their feelings and leaves their authentic self. For example, when little Johnny is hurt and goes crying to Daddy, Daddy says, "Johnny, shut up, little boys don't cry." Johnny is feeling terrified because he is really hurt, but Dad, who is three times his size, is saying that he shouldn't cry. Little Johnny, wanting to please Dad, learns to bury his hurt and pain and in some sense his authentic self with it. He develops a false self to identify with the false self of his dad. As a result Johnny smiles, even though deep down he is feeling pain.

Sadly because of hurt in childhood, many of us have left our authentic selves—our homes, and many times it is difficult to return. As one cocaine addicted person said, "Dr. Allen, I could see home but it is so hard to think of going back. The doors are broken down, the windows shut, the yard is full of weeds, and I don't think I can ever go home again. So I will just stay with cocaine." Going home is a powerful symbol for going to our inner selves. It is going through our hurt trail to touch the ground of our being—God himself. For God is our home. Psychotherapy and spiritual development can both entail a movement toward home to face exactly who we are, to be at peace with our true selves and encounter unconditional love in God—the love that will never let us go and the face that will never turn away. But going home is easier said than done. We can all identify with the old spiritual,

> Sometimes I feel like a motherless child a long, long way from home.
> Sometimes I feel like a fatherless child a long, long way from home.
> Sometimes I feel like a wandering child a long, long way from home.

Whoever we are and wherever we are, there is a longing deep in our hearts to go to a place where we feel truly accepted, loved, and trusted, a place we call home. But for many of us that place is becoming more and more unreachable and distant.

As we move into adulthood, and the onion-like layers of our false selves increase, we lose our authenticity and continue the journey of inauthenticity. We can spend our lives pleasing others; singing other people's songs, writing others' poetry, or even trying to live others' lives. As one person said, "I've had a great life, I've just never showed up for it." How tragic that the grave is filled with so many books that are unwritten or unpublished, and solutions that have never been tried. The sad thing about the false self, even though it promises to protect us from pain and actually blocks pain initially, is that ultimately it causes pain; we live below our potential and do not express the creativity that lies within us. Death is not the ultimate tragedy, because we all long for a time of rest and relief. The real tragedy is that that many of us die long before we die, because of the power of the false selves in our lives. Instead of using the talents with which we have been blessed, we allow them to rot like unpicked grapes on a vine.

The false self, which will always be with us, is only diminished when we feel loved. Whenever we feel safe in the love of someone who really cares for us, we let down our defenses and open up to face our deeper selves, our true selves. Psychotherapy involves grieving or working through our childhood trauma. As we penetrate the defenses of the false self, and expose our real, hurt selves, this in turn leads us to our deeper selves. Spirituality involves responding to God's invitation to move beyond our deeper selves, to our true selves in God. According to the Apostle Paul:

> I [my false self] have been crucified with Christ and I no longer live, but Christ lives in me. The life I [the true self] live in the body, I live by faith in the Son of God, who loved me and gave himself for me. (Galatians 2:20)

Christ put it this way, "If anyone would come after me, he must deny himself [his false self] and take up his cross and follow me" (Mark 8:34). As we work to transform our false selves, we will face our pain [our cross], but Christ is with us every step of the way.

CHARACTERISTICS OF THE FALSE SELF

The false self is a perverse rescuer. Picture a young man, hurt in childhood by the loss of his mother, and with deep feelings of rejection. He feels inadequate and finds cocaine. Finding cocaine makes him excited and euphoric. He is seduced into wanting more, but as he takes more cocaine he becomes exploited. In fact he no longer has cocaine, the cocaine has him. As he continues to take cocaine, it abandons him and eventually destroys him. Our false selves seduce us by promising relief but at the same time are exploiting us, abandoning us, and finally destroying us.

James Masterson, psychoanalyst, in his book *The Search For the Real Self* says, "The false self plays its deceptive role, ostensibly protecting us— but doing so in a way that is programmed to keep us fearful of being abandoned, of losing support or of not being able to cope on our own, not being able to be alone."[7] In *Seeds of Contemplation* Thomas Merton claims that an illusory person, the false self, who seduces us to seek for a life of pretense and illusion, shadows us.[8] For further reading look at these two books.

The following characteristics describe some attributes of the false self. You may recognize your own behavior in some of the descriptions.

Needs to please others.

Terrified at incurring the displeasure or the wrath of others, the false self will do anything to please others, developing a powerful co-dependency. This stems from a poorly developed self-image, which is compensated for by an intense desire to please others at any cost and to feel accepted at any price. Needing to please others makes it very difficult for us to let our yea be yea and our nay be nay; we hedge, waffle, and procrastinate, and sometimes remain silent for fear of rejection. The false self is preoccupied with acceptance and approval. It has a suffocating need to please others because it really cannot say no with the same confidence with which it can say yes. As a result we over-extend ourselves in relationships, projects, and courses. The false self is motivated not by personal commitment but by the fear of not living up to another's expectation.

Co-dependency may also be expressed as contra dependency in which a poor self-image, instead of having weak boundaries, is bolstered by thick, impenetrable boundaries. As a result we want other people to love and obey us even though we refuse to reciprocate. We like having them at our disposal, but we will not let them in.

Lives in fear.

The fear of abandonment, rejection, and humiliation is so effective that many of us are more influenced by fear than by love. Living by love is more open and freer but it makes us more vulnerable. Fear, on the other hand, encourages illusions, isolation, and intimacy dysfunction. With increasing threats of terrorism, crime, and violence, more people are rushing to live in the house of fear, rather than in the house of love.

Needs to appear perfect.

The false self has a compulsive desire to present an image of perfection so that everybody will admire us and nobody will know us as we really are. The illusion of perfection is a defense against the paralyzing, severe shame resulting from deprivation of the instinctual need for power and control.

Swings between elation and depression.

The false self is a perpetual roller-coaster ride of elation and depression because it is dependent on external experiences for a sense of purpose and meaning. The pursuit of money, power, glamour, sexual prowess, recognition, and status enhances our self-importance and creates the illusion of success, which can be all too easily shattered.

Skews priorities.

Focusing on what is least substantial, the false self turns away from what is real, creating a world of illusion. The Psalmist said: "How long will you love delusions and seek false gods?" (Psalm 4:2). It is very humbling to recognize that there is a tendency in our hearts to be more open to the lie or the reconstruction of reality than to accept reality itself. The false self will even seduce a person into hurting themselves, or killing others with the illusion that it will make them feel better. The false self is involved in suicide and homicide. But, perhaps most tragically, by affecting basic self-confidence, the false self has a way of producing death in the midst of life. Hence many of us, instead of attaining our full potential, spend our lives living 40 to 60 percent below our potential. Our false selves stubbornly blind us to the truth of our own emptiness or hollowness, obscuring the reality without, and preventing us from acknowledging the darkness within.

Hides inadequacy.

As we use bandages to cover physical wounds, so the false self covers our inadequacies to prevent us from being authentically observed by others. All of us have been hurt to some extent in childhood, leaving us with powerful feelings of abandonment, rejection, shame, grief and anger. The false selves developed by our brains to compensate for our childhood traumas, use such defenses as denial, pleasing others (co-dependency), blaming others (projection), workaholism and various types of addictions to cover-up our underlying hurts. It is only as we have the courage to make the journey to our hearts and face the painful experiences of our childhoods and early lives, that we can empty our hearts of pain and allow our true selves to surface and come to the forefront.

Craves compliments.

The false self must be noticed at any price. It possesses a powerful craving for compliments and pleasing behaviors, which involves us in a futile quest for some type of illusive satisfaction or fulfillment. Saint Augustine claims there can only be two basic loves—the love of God unto the forgetfulness of self; and the love of self unto the forgetfulness or denial of God.[9]

Bases its identity on relationships and achievements.

Aiming to please and to be loved at any cost, the false self is motivated to seek places of prominence to enhance a person's perceived sense of value and worth. This drive is all consuming. Success is having people liking us; conversely, failure is being rejected. In order to appreciate who we fully are in a temporal and eternal perspective, we have to be willing to be open to our relationship in God.

Is desensitised to others.

The false self is narcissistic and out of touch with our real feelings, intuitions, and insight, and so is not empathetic to the moods, needs, and dreams of others. Reciprocal sharing and intimacy are thus impossible.

According to Masterson, "It is the nature of the false self to save us from knowing the truth about our real selves, from penetrating the deeper causes of our unhappiness, from seeing ourselves as we really are—vulnerable, afraid, terrified, and unable to let our real selves emerge."[10]

Turns away from God.

Blocked from intimacy with God, ourselves, and others, the false self produces internal resistance to prayer. Creating an existential dread of silence and being alone with God, the false self specializes in trickery. It encourages laziness, distraction, and resistance in the spiritual disciplines. We are all familiar with the rationalizations that characterize our lives such as, my work is my prayer, I'm too busy to pray, I just pray when the spirit moves me. Such excuses maintain the status quo and encourage spiritual poverty and lethargy. We are made by God, for God, and nothing less than God will satisfy us. C. S. Lewis claimed that he was gripped by a desire that made everything else fade into insignificance.[11] Saint Augustine reminds us, "Our hearts will ever restless be, until we find our rest in thee."[12] Speaking of prayer, Imbach says, "Prayer is essentially the expression of our heart longing for love."[13] It is clear why the false self is one of the greatest barriers to a prayer life.

Dreads being alone.

Silence within and without is unnerving. Silence confronts the false self with its own nothingness and leads to its undoing. To avoid silence we may fill our days with activity and noise. We can arrange to be woken by a radio and drift off to sleep with a radio, driving and walking we can take our music or radio programs with us and at leisure even an uninteresting TV program or book is preferable to quietness. It is possible to live with constant noise. In the absence of background distractions, we fear being faced with our own emptiness.

Is defined by cultural values.

The false self adapts to the cultural values around us, defining us by what we have, what we do, and what others—especially significant people in our lives—think of us. As a consequence, when we lose our possessions or our reputations, ourselves are destroyed. In other words, the false self diminishes our true identity of being made in the image of God, and makes our existence conditional—based on our utility. So our worth is tied to our ever-changing, precarious life situation, rather than to the unchanging core of our God-given identity. In such a world only the strong are safe, and they are safe only as long as they have power. Since no one is strong forever, or will have power forever, no one is truly safe.

In essence, the false self is made up of what I have, what I do, and what people think of me, as guided by current cultural trends. In our Lord's earliest ministry he was challenged to develop a false self. The first temptation was to be defined by what he did: to turn stones into bread. Christ replied that human beings cannot live by bread alone but need to be empowered by God's love and word. The second temptation was to be defined by other people's opinions: to go to the top of the temple, jump down and have the angels catch him. Knowing that a nine-day wonder is just that, Christ told the evil one he should not tempt the Lord God. The third temptation was to be defined by what he had: Christ was taken up onto a mountaintop, shown the kingdoms of the world and told that if he would play the game, all power would be his. Christ made it clear that all power belongs to God (Matthew 4:1-10). As the song so poignantly says, "He's got the whole world in his hands." God alone is our center.

Sadly our life so often is off center and we live in illusion. We distract ourselves by acquiring more, doing more, and trying to be indispensable. Periodically however, quiet moments sneak up on us confronting us with the fact that underneath it all we are still poor little people who must bond with others to meet our needs.

Lives defensively.

The false self creates a fearful existence because it forces us to live defensively. We fear the loss of our possessions, our jobs, or our relationships—all of which define us in our false selves. We believe that without these things we would be nothing. Driven by fear, we can become paralyzed and unable to function normally. Ironically this in itself may result in the loss of relationships, jobs, and possessions.

Is lonely.

The false self makes the world a lonely place because we don't let others get too close to us in case they see through our false identities. If we let them come too close, they discover our lack of authenticity or emptiness, and so we keep people at a distance; this is intimacy dysfunction. The spiritual challenge is to die to this false self which we have constructed and which imprisons and forces us serve it in varying degrees of misery. Judeo Christian tradition teaches that human beings are created in the image of God. God, in essence, is the good, the true, and the beautiful; in our highest state we are reflectors of the good, the true, and the beautiful. But life is fallen and our best efforts sometimes end in failure, our best desires to do good end in doing evil; even though we want to do right, we end up doing wrong. This experience of being flawed causes us to pull away from the One who is our beginning and end: the love that never lets us go and the face that never turns away.

Why does the false self settle for life in such a diminished form? The repressed memories of childhood trauma lay the pattern for self-deception and recall faint voices from the past and vague feelings reminding us of abandonment and pain. According to Masterson, "The false self has a highly skilled defensive radar whose purpose is to avoid feelings of rejection by sacrificing the need for intimacy."[14] Masterson believes the system is constructed during the first years of life when it is important to detect what would elicit the mother's disapproval. According to Merton, the false self forms out of the cowardice of facing the fear of rejection and abandonment.[15]

VALUE OF THE FALSE SELF

As children and adolescents, we are very vulnerable and our culture makes many demands on us. The false self is an appropriate support while we are growing up. One young man who felt very inadequate had a false self that was excessively spiritual, and he immersed himself in church activities to gain the acceptance of his elders.

Brennan Manning wrote this letter when he recognized the power of his false self, that he called his impostor:

Good morning, impostor. Surely you are surprised by the cordial greeting. You probably expected, 'Hello you little jerk,' since I have hammered you from day one of this retreat. Let me begin by admitting that I have been unreasonable, ungrateful, and unbalanced in my appraisal of you. (Of course, you are aware, puff of smoke, that in addressing you, I am talking to myself. You are not some isolated, impersonal entity living on an asteroid, but a real part of me.)

I come to you today not with rod in hand but with an olive branch. When I was a little shaver and first knew that no one was there for me you intervened and showed me where to hide. (In those Depression days of the thirties, you recall, my parents were doing the best they could with what they had just to provide food and shelter.) At that moment in time, you were invaluable, without your intervention I would have been overwhelmed by dread and paralyzed by fear, you were there for me and played a crucial, protective role in my development. Thank you.

When I was four years old you taught me how to build a cottage. Remember the game? I would crawl under the covers from the head of the bed to the footrest and pull the sheets, blanket, and pillow over me—actually believing that no one could find me. I felt safe. I'm still amazed at how effectively it worked. My mind would think happy thoughts, and I would spontaneously smile and start to laugh under the covers. We built that cottage together because the world we inhabited was not a friendly place.[16]

Manning goes on to describe more of his false self, but he comes to a point where he says that even though his false self was helpful to him when he was young, protecting him from abandonment, rejection, and humiliation, as an older person he now wants to be authentic. He tells his false self it must leave. Knowing that he hurts inside and feels abandoned, rejected, and humiliated, he wants to accept these hurts, grieve through them and move on. Only by working through his pain is it possible to become open to an appreciation of his true self in God. His false self must leave so that it no longer impedes his prayer life and his understanding of who he really is. He has tried so hard to be what other people want him to be, to please people in the hope of finding peace and satisfaction. This has not worked. Now he must go home to himself, make the journey to his heart so that he can be who he essentially and authentically is. In other words, he wants to live as he will die. When we die there is nothing left but the essence of who we really are. He yearns to open up to his true self in God, the one from whom he came; the love that will never let him go, and the face that will never turn away. In life we will never be totally without our false selves, but through God's grace they can be diminished so that our true selves can see the light of day.

The rich man

A beautiful example of the false self is found in the story Jesus told of a rich man who, being financially successful, was proud of his achievements and made extensive plans to expand his operation. He fell for the illusion of permanence and ignored the fact that life is transitory; he was self-absorbed and believed he was the master and director of his fate. As a result he did it his way and planned to take his ease and live without concern for others or for God. But that night, God challenged him about his priorities, asking what use his possessions were, as he was to die that night (Luke 12:20). In other words, the rich man forgot to recognize his deeper self, his soul, which does not depend on what we possess or do. "What good is it for a man to gain the whole world, yet forfeit his soul?" (Mark 8:36). What can a person give in exchange for their soul? The false self denies the existence of the soul; it causes us to focus externally and blocks the journey to our home—our deeper selves. The hardest journey in modern society is the journey from my head to my heart.

George's story

George was an erudite and highly successful professor who had worked at the highest echelons of power in the Western world. His high-profile job came to an end and, although other opportunities were available, the loss of power and prestige were painful. Distraught and depressed he had come, as they say in the Bahamas, to the end of the road. With tears in his eyes and a deep sense of hopelessness George said, "Doc, this is my last stop. If this doesn't work I'm finished." Perplexed I asked him what he meant. Calmly and forthrightly he replied, "If this therapy doesn't work, I plan to end it all." Experience told me that he was serious.

No one truly shares their story until they feel genuinely listened to, and as I listened George poured out his heart. On a cold winter's morning he had rushed out of bed to say goodbye before his dad left for work, but to his shock and surprise, Mom and Dad were fighting. Terrified, George heard his dad tell his mother, "I don't love you anymore, and I'm leaving." Then turning to George, aged ten, who was cowering in fear and anxiety, he blurted out, "This young man is the man of the house now." According to George, at that point the ground shook under his feet—and has been shaking ever since. In an instant life became insecure and scary: the world was no longer a safe place.

From then on George's life was involved in an intense struggle to please his father. Egged on by his false self, he defended against his father's painful rejection of him by becoming extremely self-absorbed and a perfectionist. Driving himself intensely, George was rewarded with promotion after promotion until he was consulting at the pinnacle of power. Excited by his success, George would call his dad regularly to tell him about his accomplishments. Regardless of these achievements, his dad was repeatedly cold, disinterested, and rejecting. Undaunted, George continued to seek his father's approval by making special trips to visit him, but to no avail. The result was always the same.

This continual rejection by his father was hard to bear, but George claimed that the inner voices—messages from his childhood trauma—were terrifying, telling him that he was different, he was not good enough, there was something wrong with him, and that if he had been a better kid his father wouldn't have left. After work George would slump in a chair and become totally self-absorbed with these painful messages from the past. Unrested after interrupted sleep, and increasingly depressed, he threw himself into his job with ever greater determination and resolve. At work he met and fell in love with a charming lady from a prominent family. Unable to accept that he was worthy of her, he broke off the relationship. Hurt deeply by the abandonment, rejection and shame of his father's departure, George compensated with a multi-layered onion-skin-like inner self, which was manifested by self-absorption, workaholism, intimacy dysfunction and an increased addiction to seeking his father's approval in spite of the continual rejection. When George's high-powered job came to an end, he was deflated, felt like a failure, and became suicidal. In other words, his false self had seduced, exploited, abandoned, and was about to destroy him.

The pathos and pain that came through George's story were overwhelming. Asking him to describe more of what it was like as a ten-year-old when Dad left, he remembered and cried intensely saying over and over, "How could Dad leave us like that?" He said that little George must have felt abandoned and rejected, but most of all very afraid, in fact terrified. Then he recalled that after his dad left, Mom clung to him, which became a further burden. Pausing a while, I repeated how painful it must have been for the ten-year-old George to be left so callously. At this George continued to sob deeply as he was able to visualize the pain and hurt of his younger self. Asking George to keep the image of this hurt child in his mind, I asked him to imagine spending the afternoon with him. Allowing time for him to imagine them being together, I asked the older George to tell the younger George about his life since Dad left home. Overwhelmed with feelings of pain, anger, and grief, George could hardly speak. Then his words became softer and softer, eventually leading to a pregnant silence that engulfed both of us, allowing us to commune silently. At such a level words can detract from meaning and can be inadequate to express the depth of feelings repressed over the years. External silence can create internal silence, making space for recollection, the gathering together of all the fragments of the heart that have been splattered over the different surfaces of our life experience.

Easing into a gradual confrontation, I reminded George that his father rejected the younger George, leaving him stranded, to fend for himself. Then I challenged George with the question, "By threatening suicide was he not also rejecting the younger George, who was still yearning for love and attention, so repeating the cycle?" Sadly little George never had a chance to become authentic. And as a grown man, now the same age as his father was when he left home, George was refusing to re-parent little George by giving him the love he so much desired. So little George never really had a chance—nothing from nothing equals nothing.

Shocked by this interpretation of his behavior, George sat up and said, "That's not fair! I won't do that to little George." This decision led to a course of therapy over a four-year period where George worked hard at grieving his childhood pain, breaking the defensive grip of his false self on his life, and opening up to his real, hurt, but authentic self. In the second year of therapy George was able to write to his father, sharing his insights from our work together. After an agonizing month his dad wrote back asking him for forgiveness. Eventually we all met together, leading to the reconciliation of George and his father. In the fourth year of our work George became re-acquainted with his love of 11 years earlier. They were happily married and now have two children.

This story is no fairy tale where they all lived happily ever after. George continues to work on himself, facing his inner pain and dealing with ongoing conflicts to reduce the chance of his powerful false self gaining the upper hand. Life is hard; the defensive, but ever cunning, false self may be vanquished, but given half a chance rises again from the ashes like a phoenix! As with all therapy, where it ends, it only begins! The journey to authenticity is an on-going battle with and against the false self.

CONCLUSION

I cannot end this chapter without stressing how the false self weaves its way through our whole personality and life experience, and will do anything to help us defend against pain. The false self will negotiate even our own death or the death of another to make us feel better. But it is an illusion with no substance. It aims to provide emotional programs for happiness to counteract our sense of abandonment, rejection, and humiliation; but in the end it seduces us, exploits us, abandons us, and even destroys us. The Bible reminds us that "there is a way that seems right to a man, but in the end it leads to death" (Proverbs 14:12). Imprisoned in our comfortable, rational way of life, the false self blocks us from a true contemplative experience. From a psycho-spiritual perspective, one of the best ways to eliminate the false self is the practice of contemplative prayer in which the self is exposed to the naked love of God in silence. In silent prayer we change our center of gravity from our false selves to our true selves in God.

As we do this, God's spirit relates to our spirits resulting in a deep sense of peace or contemplation. Whenever we open ourselves to God, his spirit always interrelates with us whether we are aware of it or not. In this simple state of being, we consent to God's presence and action in our lives. Contemplation opens us to true communion, which often involves the mystical aspect of life; a knowing beyond knowing, a seeing beyond seeing, a hearing beyond hearing, which is nevertheless as real as the rational cognitive approach. As we combine those two forms of knowing—the cognitive and the intuitive—so we come to understand more of what it means to be a human being and we open the way to transcendence, love, freedom, inner peace, and unity in the midst of diversity.

REFERENCES

1. James Masterson, *The Search for the Real Self* (New York: Free Press, 1988), 63.

2. Brennan Manning, *Abba's Child: The Cry of the Heart for Intimate Belonging* (Colorado Springs, Colorado: Navpress, 1994), 51.

3. Thornton Wilder, *The Angel That Troubled the Waters* quoted by Brennan Manning in Abba's Child (Colorado Springs, Colorado: Navpress, 1994), 20.

4. Rainer Maria Rilke, quoted in *Psychiatry and Religion: Overlapping Concerns* by James Knight, ed Lillian Robinson, (Washington, DC: American Psychiatric Press, 1986), p.36.

5. Georges Bernanos, *Diary of a Country Priest* (New York: Sheed & Ward, 1936), 178.

6. John Bowlby, *Maternal Child Care and Mental Health,* 2nd ed. Monograph series no. 2 (Geneva: World Health Organization, 1932).

7. James Masterson, *The Search for the Real Self* (New York: Free Press, 1988), 67.

8. Thomas Merton, *Seeds of Contemplation* (New York: New Directions, 1949), 28.

9. St. Augustine, quoted by Brennan Manning in *Abba's Child* (Colorado Springs, Colorado: Navpress, 1994), 28.

10. James Masterson, *The Search for the Real Self,* quoted in *Abba's Child,* by Brennan Manning (Colorado Springs, Colorado: Navpress, 1994), 63.

11. C. S. Lewis, *Surprised by Joy* (Orlando: Harcourt Brace, 1956).

12. St. Augustine, quoted by Brennan Manning in *Abba's Child* (Colorado

Springs, Colorado: Navpress, 1994), 38.

13. Jeffrey D. Imbach, *The Recovery of Love* (New York: Crossroad, 1992), 62-63.

14. James Masterson, *The Search for the Real Self,* quoted in *Abba's Child,* by Brennan Manning (Colorado Springs, Colorado: Navpress, 1994), p38.

15. Thomas Merton, *Seeds of Contemplation* (New York: New Directions, 1949).

16. Brennan Manning, *Abba's Child: The cry of the Heart for Intimate Belonging* (Colorado Springs, Colorado: Navpress, 1994), 43.

CHAPTER 5
LECTIO DEVINA AND CONTEMPLATIVE PRAYER

Mother Teresa was asked, "How do you pray?" To which she replied, "I listen to God."
Then she was asked, "What does God do?" And she said, "He listens to me."

In recent times there has been renewed interest in Western mysticism; Christianity is looking for its own transcendent heritage. (Readers interested in the origins of Christian mysticism are referred to Andrew Louth's book.[1]) Christians are craving meditation, contemplation and depth to transcend the breakdown of society, the burgeoning influence of technology on life, and the issues and problems inherent in the creation of the global village. Whether expressed in daily conversation, the arts, the church, or corporate culture, there is little doubt that we are searching for a deeper reality at the center of things. As the poem says:

> There is a coldness in the world,
> That was not here before,
> One sees it in the sky,
> One feels it in the air,
> The trees, though root the same,
> Are somewhere far away.[2]

In essence, whatever we may choose to call it, we all have a deep yearning for God, the nameless mystery who controls the music of the spheres. Saint Augustine described a human being as a longing for God. He is our home; the love that will not let us go and the face that will never turn away.

An anonymous fourteenth century author of the book *The Cloud of Unknowing* calls us to allow all thoughts, concepts, and images to be buried beneath the cloud of forgetting, to allow our naked love to rise to the eternal God, hidden in the cloud of unknowing. [3] Interpretation of this book is complex and deeply contested, but one interpretation is that we have to move beyond our cognitive and rational concepts to realize afresh that God can only be glimpsed by love through the opening of our hearts. Rejecting all thought of what God is or what we are, we are called to become aware of who God is and who we are. Forgetting ourselves leads us to a consciousness of God, the one we love and in whom we have our being. Christian mysticism can only be understood in the context of Christ's resurrection—he alone makes us complete, "who through the Spirit of holiness was declared with power to be the Son of God by his resurrection from the dead: Jesus Christ our Lord" (Romans 1:4). When we are united with God, we are enabled to be what God wants us to be. In the incarnation God becomes one with us and in the resurrection he allows us to become like him: "I have been crucified with Christ and I no longer live, but Christ lives in me. The life I live in the body, I live by faith in the Son of God, who loved me and gave himself for me" (Galatians 2:20).

According to Thomas Merton, "The experience of contemplation is the experience of God's life and presence in ourselves as subject not as object. God is the transcendent source of our own subjectivity. Thus, contemplation is a mystery in which God reveals himself to us as the very center of our most intimate self. When the realization of his presence bursts upon us, our (false) self disappears in him and we pass mystically across the red sea of separation and find our true selves in him." [4]

How does this work in practice? Having heard the story of Jesus' interaction with Mary and Martha so many times, it was not until one Saturday morning at a Benedictine silent retreat that it was opened up to me. "The unfolding of your words gives light; it gives understanding to the simple" (Psalm 119:130). In this story Martha welcomes Jesus into their home.

Rushing around preparing the meal, Martha chastises Mary for just sitting at Jesus' feet and listening to him.

The story illustrates beautifully the difference between devotional spirituality and contemplative spirituality. In devotional spirituality we invite God into our life as a guest, and he remains a guest—we still control the reigns of our life and call the shots. Jesus becomes our gentle Jesus meek and mild, and we control, use, and sometimes abuse that reality. It's about us. It's about doing. This is the predominant spirituality that characterizes so many of our lives. Working hard and trying our best to be spiritual and caring, we strive to follow the dictates of our conscience in our worship of God, even though at times many of us are burnt out. The emphasis is on doing rather than being. We must have our devotions, we must go to church, we must serve, we must do good deeds; it all depends on us.

Martha's meal preparation was a very necessary service. I left my little island country of the Bahamas at a young age to study in Europe, and it was a wonderful blessing to be warmly welcomed into a home. Martha wanted to make Jesus feel comfortable—this was beautiful, caring, and very kind. Preparing a meal always takes time; some of us are better at it than others, but we can all thank God for those willing servants who serve us so cheerfully and so well. We are not talking about right and wrong when we compare devotional and contemplative spirituality. Devotional spirituality does much good and has brought great blessings to many; it is instrumental in furthering the kingdom of love on earth. Contemplative spirituality, on the other hand, is a grace. It is not so much something we do, but rather a place where God allows us to come with the help of his holy spirit.

We get an indication of Martha's burnout when she urges Jesus to chastise Mary for not helping with the meal, instead of dealing with Mary directly. I wonder if Martha was angry, jealous, and perhaps holding a grudge against Mary. Let's be honest, this is extremely human. After all, when we are always busy doing, we become tired and fatigued, frayed at the edges, and at times critical. Serving God is a gift, a grace. Whenever we judge others, or want to compel them to follow our way, we miss the mark. As a result, our service can become a vehicle to sanctify or vent our anger.

Contemplative spirituality, as we saw in chapter 1, has various hallmarks and is usually the sign of a mature spiritual Christian life; it is not something we can achieve, we have to allow ourselves to be known by God and to receive his grace in his time and place. In contemplative spirituality we not only invite God into our hearts as a guest, but we also bow before him and make him the host of our lives, the Lord of all. We cry from our hearts, "thou alone dwells here". You plus me always equal two, but in contemplative spirituality, you plus God always equal one because our small I becomes a part of the great I am. Our being lives in his eternal being, yet in the mystery of it all I retain my personality, God respects my identity and does not want an automaton.

Mary was given the mystical grace of contemplation. Sitting at Jesus' feet, Mary listened attentively to him. Using repetition, Jesus called Martha's name twice, saying that she was worried and troubled about too many things; she was distracted. These loving words to Martha also speak directly to us. In this modern culture many of us find ourselves rushing to-and-fro, we live distracted lives, and find it very difficult to make time to nurture our inner lives, to open ourselves to God's love. Ignoring our spouses, neglecting our children, withdrawing from friends, we have no time—life becomes a mad rush. It is difficult to receive the gift of contemplative prayer while living a rushed lifestyle. In contemplative prayer God alone is the focus; we willingly consent to God's presence and action in our lives.

This is more easily said than done, because of our need for action and our desire to defend against the childhood traumas of abandonment, rejection, and humiliation. As we wait in silence before God, listening or waiting for him, we have to let go of our defenses and open ourselves to his pure love. It seems to me that Martha approached faith from the outer or external perspective and neglected the inward aspects. Conversely, in contemplation we start inward and move out. The psalmist David said, "surely you desire truth in the inner parts" (Psalm 51:6). Jesus taught that, in spite of there being so much to distract and involve us, only one thing is needful—to be open to the experience of God's love and healing in the world, infusing our life with grace, creativity, and hope.

Life is about growing our souls, the only things we can take with us when we leave this world. As Jesus said to Martha, "Mary has chosen what is better, and it will not be taken away from her" (Luke 10:42). He emphasized that human beings cannot live by bread alone but depend on the love that comes from God, "What good is it for a man to gain the whole world, yet forfeit his soul?" (Mark 8:36). What can a person give in exchange for their soul? Our inner life only develops by the witness of God's spirit through his love for us. This is no quick fix; it takes time, patience, and commitment.

Contemplative prayer is sitting at Jesus' feet, moving beyond our thoughts, images, and feelings, being open to the pure, naked love of God. Being in the presence of God to receive of his spirit always gives life: "the words I have spoken to you are spirit and they are life" (John 6:63). Contemplation is the transformation of consciousness in which God takes his place at the apex of our lives. His eternal love not only touches our own hearts but also reaches out through us to others and to the world around us. When God's people are channels of his love for those around them, the whole world becomes pregnant with God—with the vision and presence of God's love in the world. Contemplative prayer is a process through which knowing God is experienced. In fact it is really hard for us to know God; contemplative prayer essentially means that we allow God to know us by dropping our resistances and opening our hearts. By working through our hurt and pain we allow God's love to penetrate us. Contemplative prayer is a commitment, but it is also a gift.

Much has been written about the importance of contemplation, and I have found *Seeds of Contemplation* by Thomas Merton [5] and *Out of Solitude* by Henri Nouwen6 especially helpful. Life is wounded and our center of gravity tends to be focused in our false or defensive self. But in contemplative prayer we open to God, allowing our center of gravity to move from our false selves to our true selves in God. I believe that when we commit to listening to God's word and sitting in silence in the naked presence of God's love, his spirit unites with our spirits and contemplation always occurs. Obviously there are times when we are conscious of what's going on, but in my experience it often seems as if nothing is happening. God's spirit witnesses to our spirits that we belong to him and as it says in Romans 8:26, "We do not know what we ought to pray for, but the Spirit himself intercedes for us with groans that words cannot express." In essence then, although God gives us the gift of contemplation, it is only by practice and commitment that we receive the grace of the awareness of union with God. In union with God we do not lose our personality but become more fully a person. When a log is placed on a fire, it burns and becomes one with the fire, although it is still a log. Like the log, we are transformed.

IMPORTANCE OF COMMITMENT

Contemplative prayer requires commitment. According to psychotherapist Victor Franco, a person finds identity only to the extent that he commits himself to something beyond himself, to a cause greater than himself.[7] Many of us rarely find something of depth to commit ourselves to and as a result we never seem to get beneath the surface of our lives and often die even before we live.

It is important to understand that contemplative prayer is more a prayer of intention than attention. It is seeking God without a specific agenda—a prayer of commitment and a consent that God, through his grace and spirit, may work in us. Recognizing this, the apostle says that God's spirit prays continually in us with words that cannot be uttered (Romans 8:26). So, in a very deep sense, contemplative prayer is where we open our hearts in silence to God to allow the prayer of God to continue in our lives. But even though we practice the prayer perhaps twice a day, it is so important to note that the prayer of God continues throughout our lives, twenty-four hours a day. As we practice contemplative prayer, through God's grace, we become more aware of the prayer of God taking place in our lives. When this occurs there is a parallel experience of God's presence that always involves his love, peace, and joy.

Opening ourselves to contemplative prayer, the interaction with God leaves us passionate in his presence. Passion, derived from the Latin word for suffer, implies waiting, so as we open ourselves to contemplative prayer there is a deep sense of passionate waiting for God's love to involve us, hold us, and bless us. Passion is not just high emotion, but a deep determination and a deep commitment to stay centered in the awareness of faith. As we open to contemplative prayer and become more passionate, in my experience we also become more compassionate; we move inwardly to touch the very presence, or realm, of God's love in our lives. Occurring at the time of prayer, this interaction is only validated as we get up from prayer and move into the world. In other words, the deep passion that occurs in contemplative prayer is validated by the compassion shown from our lives towards others and the world without. Hence, we then follow the example of God, who is the lover, who keeps moving toward us, the beloved, in spite our pain, our woundedness, and our struggles of knowing and being known.

CONTEMPLATION AND PASSION

I have been blessed by the work of Father Joseph Chu-Cong who has written so beautifully about the relationship between contemplation, erotic love, and spiritual union. According to Father Cong, contemplation is the spark of life that allows us to walk in deep friendship and love with God, each other, and nature. He reminds us that in contemplation there are periods of dullness, dryness and frustration along with times of intimacy and communion. Contemplation, resulting from the practice of contemplative prayer, is a powerful force for healing and producing intimacy in a distant world.[8] Father Cong reminds us that some of the great saints of the past placed much emphasis on the overwhelming power of nature to reflect the glory of God. According to Cong, Francis of Assisi scolded the flowers saying, "Be quiet, be quiet! You speak of my Beloved. It is too much for me." [9] And then Saint Bernard of Clairvaux, (who first described the concept of the false self (chapter 4)), overwhelmed by God's presence in his creation, says: "God is the stone in the stones, the tree in the trees." According to Saint Bernard, God resides in the heart of all that exists, from the most interior to the most visible. Confiding in a close friend, Saint Bernard says, "Believe me as one who has experience, you will find much more among the woods than you would ever find among books."[10] This deep contemplation also occurs in literature, as when Shakespeare writes, "Tongue in trees, books in the running brooks, servants and stones and good in everything"[11] and Gerard Manley Hopkins says, "The world is charged with the grandeur of God."[12] And of course we have a deep contemplative experience expressed by some of the Zen masters. For example, "When one's mind is religiously awakened, one feels as though in every blade of wild fern or solid stone is something really transcendent."[13] Father Cong, who himself was brought up in a very strict Christian monastic tradition, later rediscovered the deep spirituality reflected in the solution of what he described as the *Zen cone*. "Empty hand yet holding a hoe! Walking yet riding a water buffalo."[14] On the surface this statement is paradoxical. How can we be empty handed and still hold a hoe? How can we be walking and still riding a water buffalo? But in the contemplative experience paradox is diminished. Although our hearts may be empty, yet because of God's love we are filled and empowered to do his work, that is holding a hoe. Even though we walk we are graced with God's presence, which allows us to rise up with wings as eagles, walk and not faint, run and not be weary (Isaiah 40:31). In contemplation we can experience the reality of our intimate union with God, a relationship in which we are deeply loved.

Recognized as a gem in the literature of the Judeo Christian mystical traditions, the Song of Songs is an authoritative treasury of words and images for the contemplative experience.

> I belong to my lover,
> and his desire is for me.
> Come, my lover, let us go to the countryside,
> let us spend the night in the villages (Song of Songs 7:10-11).

In both the East and the West the Song of Songs is revered because of its profundity and boldness, but many of us modern readers cannot see further than a celebration of the joys of sensual love. On a deeper level the Song of Songs deals with the transformation of human erotic and sensual desire to experience a deeper union with God. Eros, known as the life force, is usually equated with erotic love but according to Saint John Climacus, a sixth century mystic theologian, "When we love God with the strength of Eros, the Eros is transformed into agape, the spiritual love that comes from above."[15] Eros, yearning or passionate love, is an authentic starting point for understanding communion with God.

A profound sense of intimacy is expressed in the concept of the Eucharist—Christ asked us to do this in remembrance of him. As we partake of the bread, his body, and drink of the wine, his blood, we are intimately related to him and to all the pilgrims on the spiritual journey, both past, present, and future. The Eucharist, the Lord's Supper, is an integral part of understanding the depth of contemplation, and opening to the grace of contemplative prayer. This became very obvious to me at the time of my mother's death in 1977. Her funeral was planned for 3 p.m. that Sunday afternoon and the Eucharist was to be held at 11a.m. Overwhelmed by grief and sadness, I thought it best to rest in the morning and prepare myself to attend the funeral at 3 p.m. But during my time of contemplative prayer I became aware that, in a mystical way, I would be closer to my mother during the Eucharist than perhaps at her funeral, for in the Eucharist we experience the presence of Christ and the communion of all the saints.

Another example that stays deeply with me is memories of the beautiful Eucharists held on Maundy Thursday by the late Father Henry Nouwen in the little chapel at Yale Divinity School. The chapel was very simple, the alter was bare, and Father Nouwen would sit with us and speak gently and lovingly of the love of Christ. He talked about the importance of abiding in Christ and Christ abiding in us, and as he broke the bread, the body of Christ, and we shared the wine, the blood of Christ, there was a powerful sense of connection and community along with a deep sense of intimacy. Even now, looking back, the presence of Christ was very real.

Such experiences indicate a powerful sense of intimacy in our distant world; very simple, yet so profound. I know that Nouwen, like all of us, struggled terribly with intimacy and closeness in his prayer life. Intimacy and authenticity are not a constant state of being here in this vale of tears, but are a dynamic process in our struggle in prayer to draw near to God, ourselves, others and the cosmos. The Psalmist described it so well when he said, "when I awake, I will be satisfied with seeing your likeness" (Psalm 17:15). Similarly, the apostle Paul said, "Now we see but a poor reflection as in a mirror; then we shall see face to face. Now I know in part; then I shall know fully, even as I am fully known" (1 Corinthians 13: 12).

Contemplation is based on the fact that God, who is love, loves us with a love more powerful than death, and nothing can separate us from this love. To experience the love of God is not some hypothetical or sentimental experience, but rather a vision of God's love in the world manifested by a deep commitment to carry out the mission of his love and compassion. At times the vision is blurred and often the mission unfocused, but the practice of contemplative prayer clarifies the vision and allows us to become reconnected or refurbished in the mission. Contemplation then is a powerful transformation of consciousness, where we open to God's love and his expression in the world around us—in our work, our play, our family time, our community, or enjoying the beauty of nature. Love makes one of us all. It provides a deep sense of unity in the midst of diversity. After all, we come from love, for love, and return to love. Contemplation is completing the circle of God's love to us. As we open ourselves to contemplative prayer, the divine energy expresses itself by lighting up the darkness of the world around us, allowing us to see the beauty that existed all along. T. S. Eliot so beautifully describes this,

> We shall not cease from exploration,
> And the end of all of our exploring
> Will be to arrive where we started,
> And know the place for the first time.[16]

Slowly but surely, as contemplation begins to take hold of all aspects of our lives, we begin to see as God sees; we begin to listen as God listens. So the ordinary things that we take so often for granted speak to us of his love and his peace and become emblazoned with a new sense of excitement, adventure, and meaning.

A METHODOLOGY OF CONTEMPLATIVE PRAYER

Contemplation is the mystery of the encounter, or dare I say the romance, between human beings and God. In the early chapters of Genesis, Adam and Eve, our representatives, stood in the presence of God and talked with him. Then destruction in paradise changed this beautiful relationship. "The man and his wife heard the sound of God walking in the cool of the day and then hid from God among the trees of the garden, but God called to man, 'Where are you?'" (Genesis 3:9). After the fall God spoke to us through prophets, in many other ways, and then through his son, Jesus Christ. The communion and conversation between God and human beings continues. Contemplative prayer represents that on-going communion and requires commitment to be open to God not just during the time of prayer but throughout each moment of our lives. Please note that this section is called *A Methodology*. It is just that: one methodology that you may find helpful.

Influenced by the writings of Basil Pennington and others, when I speak of contemplative prayer I am really talking of Lectio Devina. Developed by a twelfth century Carthusian monk called Guigo, it is

known as Guigo's ladder, and is divided into four stages, four ways of
reading a passage:

1. reading or *lectio,*
2. meditation or *meditatio,*
3. oral prayer or *oritorio,* and
4. silent prayer or *contemplatio.*

Later a fifth stage *operatio* was added—the idea of incarnating the
reading into our daily experience. This is a refinement of the four aspects
of scripture commonly found in the traditions of the early fathers of the
church. Each rung of the ladder corresponds to a different level of spiritual
understanding. Father Cong describes the Lectio Devina as relating to
these four aspects of literature:

1. literal—sacred reading, attending to the words of the passage;
2. moral—meditation, reasoning as we search and inquire to see
what the text has to say about our lives;
3. allegorical—oral prayer, experiencing the reality of God's
love as we look into the text, deepening our faith and response
to God's love;
4. mystical—contemplation, listening as God the Holy Spirit
speaks to us in the quietness of our hearts, bathing us afresh in his
love, renewing our spirits, giving us courage and hope to
continue with our lives. [17]

The vision of God and the mission of God's love in the world must
always balance contemplation. This is the fifth stage, operatio. Moses was
called to the mountaintop to experience the vision of God, but he had to
return to the valley to serve the people, that is the mission of God's love
in the world. True contemplation always leads to compassion, it essentially
means going to the mountaintop...to return to wash the feet of our brothers and sisters. Contemplation is best summed up in the beautiful words of
Elizabeth Barrett Browning, "Earth's crammed with heaven and every common bush alive with God and only he who sees takes off his shoes; the
rest sit round 'and pluck blackberries'."[18]

In preparation for the time of contemplative prayer it is important to
have a few moments of silence to quiet or center ourselves, by breathing
deeply or other simple relaxation exercises. Dedicating it to a particular
person or situation focuses our time of prayer. Having a defined space can
also be helpful to enhance the practice of our prayer. The place becomes

sanctified, in a sense we bring the presence of God to the place, but in an interesting way the place also brings the presence of God to our experience. So often our prayers, no matter how genuine, tend in our audible or inaudible reflection to defend against the pain and hurt in our hearts. The practice of Lectio Devina is a way of putting our own agenda to one side. As we read God's word the Holy Spirit of God in the word communes with the spirit in us, and allows us to be open to God and the reading. We can then be open to him in the reflection, speak to him from our hearts, but then most importantly listen and let him speak to us, "with groans that words cannot express" (Romans 8:26). The real test of this experience is then leaving the prayer and moving out into the world to show the compassion to ourselves, others, and the world around us.

1. Lectio, reading (the literal)

The one-year Bible is a very helpful way to do the reading, because it provides passages from the Old Testament, the New Testament, the Psalms, and the Proverbs throughout the year. Reading should be repetitive so that our hearts are saturated with God's words; we not only read the text, it also reads us and the spirit of God will emphasize or point out a particular verse or phrase or word. It is important that we see this word or phrase as God's gift to us for that particular day and make it our act of prayer— reflect on it and to repeat it throughout the day. I find that I very easily forget, and so I encourage writing down the phrase or word and referring to it during the day. The spirit of God in us is the same spirit that wrote the word and when the two come together they bare witness to each other and give us guidance through the day.

I cannot stress how important it is to cherish the word that is given as a gift, a grace provided by God, to remind us of his love throughout the whole day. We all have favorite passages that mean so much to us; for example, Psalm 23, 1Corinthians 13, John 3 verses 1-16, Matthew 5, Isaiah 6, John 13 and John 20 and so on. We may also find it helpful to read certain inspired readings; for example, Henry Nouwen's *The Return of the Prodigal Son*.19 As we read let us be grasped by the central ideas presented and recognize and question what God is saying to us. Many times in the spiritual journey we have to be satisfied with various questions that eventually grow into responses. This is at odds with our reductionist society, which demands immediate answers. The spiritual journey is a path of waiting patiently, but waiting in love and hope.

2. Meditatio, reflection (the moral)

Examining the text to clarify what God has said to us, we use our minds as well as our hearts to explore the meaning for our own lives. As we listen deeply to the particular words or verse we find ourselves being confronted with different thoughts and questions. It is helpful to reflect on these thoughts by writing them down. Be careful not to be seduced by purely discursive reasoning, but simply let the text speak to us by abiding in it. Listen to the words as if they were directly spoken to us. Believing that God is speaking to us personally through the word or text allows us to open our hearts in adoration and wonder so that we are penetrated by his awareness and this encourages our growth in contemplation. The word becomes a living part of us, revealing God's truth as a mirror reveals our external appearance. Spiritual truths along with moral values illuminate our weaknesses and often convince us of our woundedness and failures. An awareness of our infidelities and sins causes us to pray for the courage to live like David, who was confronted with stern words of rebuke about his immoral behavior by Nathan, the prophet (2 Samuel 12:1-13). But God always gives grace, for he is merciful and long suffering. As deep reflection grows in our hearts, the spirit will give life and light to guide us on our way. Like the Blessed Virgin Mary, we will ponder the words of God in our hearts (Luke 2:19).

3. Oritorio, oral prayer (the allegorical)

Praying dispels the opacity of life so that we see God's love and peace in action through the day. This deepens our faith and responsiveness. Verbal prayer should be concise; the longer the prayer the more we find ourselves falling back into our false mind-made selves to defend against our early childhood pain of abandonment, rejection, and humiliation. Keeping our prayers short and to the point enables us to commune more directly with God. Remember that we are more blessed by what God has to say to us than by what we have to say to him. But more than that, we are more healed by what he says to us than by what we say to him.

4. Contemplatio, contemplation (the mystical)

Contemplation is the awareness of God that takes us beyond all dualistic thinking, and which allows us to find ourselves alone with the Alone where we are truly real. For example, we can't fill a bottle with good wine, if it is already full of spoiled wine. First we have to empty out the spoiled wine. So, by working through our hurts in therapy or prayer, we have to empty ourselves of the false illusory selves—so that God can fill us with himself and allow us to find love in the meaning of our true selves in him. According to Shannon "when this happens in death, we experience heaven, but when this happens in life, we receive contemplation."[20] The awareness of God (the vision of God) is not some sentimental mumbo jumbo experience but is validated in our daily commitment to the mission of God's love in the world—as we reach out in love to our brother and sister, and care for the environment.

In contemplation we experience what it means to be open to the presence of God, allowing his spirit to pray in us as God's spirit dwells in us, "Do you not know that your body is a temple of the Holy Spirit?" (1 Corinthians 6:19). This extremely humbling mystical aspect of contemplation draws us into the silence of God's presence. Remaining silent for twenty minutes or half an hour, we open ourselves to be bathed in the naked love of God. In my experience it takes 10 to 15 minutes for the traffic in our heads to settle and so half an hour may be more appropriate. External silence leads to interior silence, creating a sense of stillness and space to listen to God. It is in this space, this stillness and quietness that we sit at the table spread for two, God and ourselves. But since God is the father of the eternal brotherhood, where we meet God in ourselves we somehow also touch the souls of our brothers and sisters. In a mystical way, through the process of silent contemplation we find a powerful intimacy in a so-called distant world. David speaks of this so beautifully; "You prepare a table before me in the presence of my enemies" (Psalm 23:5). During silence the mind breaks the obsession with attachment to our pathological narcissism, where we spend 24 hours a day focused on ourselves, and opens us up to the healing presence of God's love. Breaking the attachment to our reductionist narcissistic selves is not easy. Choosing a holy word draws us quietly back to our focus on God's presence.

According to the author of *The Cloud of Unknowing:*

> If you want to gather all your desire into one simple word
> that the mind can retain, choose a short word rather than
> a long one. A one-syllable word such as "God" is best, but
> choose one that is meaningful to you and fix it in your
> mind so that it will remain there all day. The word will be
> your defense in conflict and in peace. Use it to beat upon
> the cloud of darkness above you and subdue all the
> distractions consigning them to the cloud of forgetting
> beneath you. Should some thought go on annoying you,
> demanding to know what you are doing, answer with this
> one word alone, if your mind begins to intellectualize of
> the meaning and connotations of this little word, remind
> yourself that its value lies in its simplicity. Do this and I
> assure you your thoughts will vanish.[21]

Using the word *Lord* exposes us to the power of the Lord Jesus
Christ's incarnation, life, death, and resurrection. Expelling the forces of
darkness and the negative forces so often present in our life and around
us, it opens us to the glorious light of God's presence. *I find The Jesus
Prayer* also helpful: "God, have mercy on me, a sinner" (Luke 18: 13). Many
times when I am stressed and finding it difficult to concentrate, I begin
with this prayer, focusing silently on it and holding on to the word 'Lord'
to help the silent contemplation. Each person must arrive in silence to recognize that God is praying in us. It is the pathological connection to our
selfishness and the things we are attached to, that prevent us from opening to the pure presence of God's love, healing, and grace in our lives. It
may be helpful to prepare for the silence by taking three deep breaths,
held to the count of four, to allow the body to relax. Please do not be discouraged, if twenty minutes is too long to start with, you can build up to
this. Remember a learning curve is involved.

The psalmist claims that he learned to calm and quiet his spirit (Psalm
131:2). He said, as a mother holds her newly born baby, he has learned to
calm and quiet his soul. It does take time to learn how to be quiet. When
our minds wonder through thoughts, feelings, or images, we can let these
float away like ships blown across the sea. When our minds wonder, we

just silently return to our holy word and focus back on the presence of God. In the Bahamas I find looking at the ocean a great illustration of contemplation; as different boats pass by in front of me, I can still focus on the ocean. Similarly, in contemplative meditation, as various thoughts sail by we should let them go and focus our awareness on being in God's presence.

The period of silence falls into two or three categories. First comes recollection or catching ourselves, restoring the split parts of our hearts. Like the psalmist we say "Teach me your way, O Lord, and I will walk in your truth; give me an undivided heart, that I may fear your name" (Psalm 86:11). Secondly there is the time of quiet prayer when our hearts become very still. Thirdly is the experience of ecstasy. Depending on God's grace and time we may experience being caught up with him in a very beautiful way, outside of ourselves. Remember this is only a peek experience and cannot be prolonged but it does happen and can be very meaningful. However, the classic authors, including the Cloud author stressed that such experiences were not to be sought, and were not the goal of contemplation.

It is so important for us to remember that prayer is all about God and not about us. It has to do with God completing his work in us, with allowing the Holy Spirit to pray in us. It is difficult for us not to judge our experience of contemplation, allowing our false selves to introduce a powerfully competitive spirit. In fact it is impossible to judge prayer. Contemplation is giving our consent to God to do his work in us.

5. Operatio, action (the outworking)

Operatio means opening to our lives. Armed with the healing word or phrase, we go into the throws of everyday life expecting to experience the grace of God in every incident, situation, or person we encounter. Contemplative prayer does not end when the silence is broken, but continues throughout the day. At midday it is helpful to stop and have a time of quiet to recall the verse or phrase that one was given during the devotional period in the morning. It may be helpful to repeat a summary of the Lectio Devina sometime in the early evening, again including twenty minutes of silent prayer; some people find that this is too stimulating to do late night, but the goal is to pray whenever we can find time to do so.

As we go through the day, prayer is opening to the presence of God as we encounter individuals in difficult circumstances or are touched by the beauty and wonder of nature so that the world becomes pregnant with God. As we make a habit of the prayer life, periodically we may be awakened during the night. Do not be discouraged by this for it is a special grace given to us to spend time with God; he is the lover who is always seeking us, the beloved. It may be appropriate to dedicate the time of silence to a person who is in need or in a difficult situation.

Preparing our hearts for sleep is important. Saint Augustine prayed that God would purify his dreams. In the rush of modern life we have lost the meaning of dreams, but God speaks through dreams and as we open to a contemplative lifestyle the recovery of our dreams may occur. By recording our dreams we then have a leading of the Spirit to understand them. It is important to note that even though we may go to a therapist, the interpretation of the dream, what God is saying to us, is our responsibility. For each heart knows its pain, and each heart knows its joy.

DYNAMICS OF CONTEMPLATION

Contemplation is a transformation of consciousness through which we come to a deeper understanding of the vision of God's love, which is then manifested in a total commitment to the mission of God's love and compassion in the word. The mission of love always involves self-development, the caring or the formation of community, and an informed understanding and stewardship of God's love in the world.

Contemplation is an expression of the deep relationship between God, the Holy other, and finite human beings. It is manifest in loving concern for the self, each other, and the world. The dynamics of contemplation, like those of intimacy, includes the stages of attraction, fusion, crisis, commitment, intimacy, and union.[22]

Attraction

A call to contemplation comes from God, and so God always initiates the attraction to contemplation. It is a gift—a grace, because God the lover seeks us the beloved. "I belong to my lover, and his desire is for me" (Song of Songs 7:12-13). Not that we first love God but that he first loved us. We can never move beyond the presence of God, although we can be without the awareness of him. So, when we move toward God we have an increased awareness that is manifested by a desire for his presence, a deeper love for forgiveness, and the recognition that God is our basic yearning.

Fusion

As we respond to God's love in our life by committing ourselves to the practice of Lectio Devina and contemplative prayer, we experience a deep sense of peace, excitement, and calm. We long for this wonderful experience to continue forever, to make it permanent, like Peter on the mount transfiguration wanting to build three shelters (Mark 9:5). As with all deep intimate experiences, during fusion our ego boundaries break down leading to a sense of ecstasy. But fusion is only temporary. After birth a child fuses to its mother; but if the child remains fused it does not develop, and may become severely emotionally damaged. So fusion is temporary and in order to grow up our ego boundaries snap back into position, starting us on the way to separation or individuality, and we enter the stage of crisis. In the same way, Peter found that the transfiguration was supposed to be a short-lived, peak experience out of which they were to return to serve the people (Mark 9:5-9).

Crisis

Crisis in the spiritual journey is always difficult. Our prayer life dries up. We lose enthusiasm. Some of us try to self-soothe with sex, alcohol, a new church, or a new form of prayer. We try to pray but it seems as if heaven is sealed over and our prayers are blocked. As we struggle to keep up the practice of our prayer life, it almost seems as if God has hidden himself from us and our prayers reach no further than the ceiling. Our hearts become cold and we suffer an intense interior aloneness and frustration. God has said that he will never leave us (Isaiah 41:10), but maybe sometimes his presence is so dazzling that we cannot see him, and so experience a sense of darkness. As with a child fused to its mother, we need to move on from fusion in order to grow, and often we grow through crisis.

In this time of emptiness and dryness in our prayer lives, and amidst the pain of life and crushing problems, our false selves cause us to seek happiness by gratifying our basic instinctual needs for survival-security, affection-esteem, power and control. Our false selves base their worth on cultural conditioning and group identification—they become empowered during this difficult time and our prayer lives are in jeopardy. We try to find fulfillment through our jobs, possessions, pleasures, addictions, and by exerting control over those we live or work with. When we are frustrated in this, we experience the so-called afflicted emotions: sadness, grief, anger, fear, guilt, shame, humiliation, and despair. Our internal messages can tie us into emotional knots—leading to destruction or the development of self-soothing practices involving, as I said before, drugs, alcohol, sex, or maybe even church. It is so important to remember that the suffering of crisis is never an end in itself—with God's grace it is a stepping-stone to transformation. The only antidote to crisis in our prayer lives is complete faithfulness and resistance. As we continue to open ourselves to God, he then continues to reveal himself to us.

Persistence

Our natural tendency in the face of crisis is to flip back into our addictive self-images and familiar old self-soothing patterns. However, we can take as our model Mary Magdalene at the tomb of Jesus; she just stayed there. It was painful, but she stayed there. She was alone, but she stayed there. It seemed as if the situation was hopeless, but she stayed there. She was told that in some sense Christ was not there, but she stayed there. The disciples, on visiting the tomb and finding Christ raised, left; but Mary stayed there. The only way out of the crisis is a determined commitment to the word of God in silence. "Be still," says the psalmist, "and know that I am God" (Psalm 46:10). Contemplation requires that we learn to be faithful, to hold our ground, and to stay there. Of course during this time we miss the presence of our Lord, but remember that we can only miss somebody whom we know and love. And so, in essence then, the very missing of the presence of Christ is an indication that we are in relationship with him.

Union

As we persevere in the practice of contemplative prayer, recollection—withdrawing our hearts from all their attachments and turning our love to God—becomes easier. We will still have ups and downs and difficult times, but periodically God's grace gives us a peak or peek experience and we are surprised by joy; this is a taste of heaven. But remember it is only a peek, and before long we are sent back down to continue in the mission of love in the world. The Magi in T. S. Elliot's poem returned from their wonderful, life-changing experiences and knew that they would never be the same again:

> We returned to our places, these Kingdoms,
> But no longer at ease here, in the old dispensation,
> With an alien people clutching their Gods.[23]

So in our own experience, as we open ourselves to the revolutionary experience of contemplative prayer, we will notice that the things that once we were attached to and that controlled our lives, have less power as we seek the love that will not let us go and the face that never turns away. Know that love and contemplation are the language and activity of heaven, and earth is the souls' apprenticeship or gymnasium for heaven. We are all lovers, mystics, and contemplatives; contemplative prayer helps to develop an awareness of who we are as children of God, why we are here. It opens us up to the divine destiny to which we are called: prayer as a relationship, not a recitation, a partnership with the Lord that grows, a friendship with the Lord that grows in love. Contemplative prayer awakens the eyes of the heart to see the world as God sees it. As God becomes more present, we recognize the divine in our brothers and sisters, we see God in the world beneath and beyond ordinary circumstances. Christ referred to this union with God when he said, "Come to me, all you who are weary and burdened, and I will give you rest" (Matthew 11:28). The full realization that the all-powerful creator loves us to such an extent that he makes us co-workers with him is humbling indeed. In contemplative prayer, the more we become whole, the more we become holy. We desire prayer not for itself, but so that we have the strength to serve and to open our hearts to express God's purpose and love in the world.

In essence, then, in union with God we experiencing contemplative prayer to be the loving gaze of God upon our souls as we sit in adoration. As the psalmist said,

> One thing I ask of the Lord, this is what I seek:
> that I may dwell in the house of the Lord
> all the days of my life,
> to gaze upon the beauty of the Lord and to seek
> him in his temple (Psalm 27:4).

SOME RESULTS OF CONTEMPLATIVE PRAYER

We have to be extremely careful here, because prayer can never be utilitarian. We just pray, we do not ask whether we pray well or whether we pray poorly, but as we persist in contemplative prayer there are a number of blessings that God, through his loving kindness, bestows upon us.

Broadening spirituality

An early and important insight that results from our prayer life is that our spirituality broadens out—we open ourselves to seeing God's presence in all persons and situations, and experience the infinite freedom of his love. In truth, authentic spirituality is the expansion of the inner self, that is the soul, to a limitless universe. As it says in Genesis, "God saw all that he had made, and it was very good" (Genesis 1:31). In reality, because life is wounded, this awareness is not complete, and our false selves can easily block it out as they seek to defend us against the pains of life.

Seeing through God's eyes

Contemplative prayer gives us an ability to see the good in spite of the pain in the world. As we persist in prayer we begin to see as God sees. So often in our human existence, we just see with the eyes physiologically, but when we pray we see with the eyes of the heart and come to understand and recognize the importance of the Eternal God's perspective. And sometimes, through his spirit, we are given a panoramic view of how the past, present, and future relate. Contemplatives become citizens of both earth and heaven, not seeing from a purely temporal perspective, but also from a heavenly perspective.

Loving creation

Contemplative prayer gives us a deep love and appreciation for the created world. In spite all of the crises and natural disasters that occur, our prayer life yields us the perception to see that "Holy, holy, holy is the Lord Almighty; the whole earth is full of his glory" (Isaiah 6:3). In spite of the problems and pain of life, the glory of God is spread through the earth.

Opening to the kingdom

Contemplative prayer prepares us for the kingdom of God. In opening ourselves to be in God's presence with our consent that he do his work in us, we really open ourselves to the presence of the kingdom of God and we pray "your kingdom come, your will be done on earth as it is in heaven" (Matthew 6:10). For the Kingdom of God is within us (Luke 17:21).

Finding direction

Contemplative prayer gives the soul a sense of direction and fulfillment through the deeper shedding of our heart. Looking at our fairy tales and myths, we talk of the transformation of dragons or of the beast in Beauty and the Beast and of the lost princess in Cinderella. We have this dream of being somewhere where all is fine and all is well. Contemplation opens us to the joys of heaven even though we are still presently on the earth. It increases our awareness of God but also God's presence. Wherever God really is we are safe because, "if God is for us, who can be against us?" (Romans 8:31).

Healing from addiction

Contemplation particularly allows us to awaken from a life of addiction to live in a life of love which is ever opening and ever developing, involving our own self-development, a movement in community toward others and a deep caring for the world. Connected to this is a new appreciation of mystery. So often we make God very familiar and we forget that the Apostle Paul said, "the mystery of godliness is great" (1 Timothy 3:16). There is so much we don't understand; coming to contemplation we must come with a sense of humility and a sense of basic trust but also with hope.

Growing in understanding

It is important to note although contemplation improves our relationship with God, it does not immunize us or protect us from the pain and suffering of life. But it does help us to grow in understanding and to see things from a divine perspective. This makes all the difference because we come to recognize that the same God that is in us is also in the world.

Being changed

And finally, contemplative prayer really calls us to the experience of being alone with God. As Christ said, "when you pray, go into your room, close the door and pray to your Father, who is unseen" (Matthew 6:6). We are called to come alone and to come apart and to bolt our hearts from all of the contaminating experiences of our present life. So contemplative prayer really calls for a deep intimate relationship with God. We sit at the table set for two, God and us. This inner table of course is associated with inner space where we learn to let go, to experience a deep calm, incredible stillness, and a cosmic silence beyond time. It is a dimension of our interconnectedness with divinity and each other—the nonverbal communing of saints. As we open ourselves to contemplative prayer our human spirits immerse themselves in the living water; we emerge cleansed and refreshed with progressive healing of our inner wounds. Each time we surface we are different people, because in the presence of the Almighty's creative power a change takes place in our hearts; we begin to see more deeply, to hear more astutely, our actions becomes more focused. This union with God develops a sense of wonder, and we look afresh at every person, at nature, and at the universe. We experience God at the heart of all creation.

Glimpsing heaven

And perhaps the most exciting of all, contemplation really is a peek into the beyond. A reminder that we are only passing through an earthly journey going to a home beyond this place and so we are reminded that we are seated in the heavens (Ephesians 2:6). This recognition that our lives have at least two dimensions—on earth, to further our work here, but also the eternal perspective which will influence our work in this present world. Like everything else in life, we could talk or write pages of theoretical understandings of various concepts, particularly the concept of prayer, but in essence the meaning of prayer is that it must be expressed in a practical way.

She was a very lovely lady, the mother of two children, married to a young lawyer in a very busy metropolitan area. They were as you say, making it and of course the price of making it in our modern world and living in such an area is a very fast pace of life—sometimes with economic difficulties or trouble finding baby sitters. And so the wife, feeling somewhat isolated and rejected, felt discouraged and became depressed. The depression continued and eventually she started to develop panic attacks where she felt terrified of being at home with the children. Being a believer, she read the scripture, attended church faithfully, and sought help. She told me that she came from a very contemplative background—during the Eucharist people would sit and meditate on the meaning of Christ's suffering, death, and resurrection. But somehow the hustle and bustle and the urgent time pressures of a metropolitan lifestyle had knocked this out of her and she felt adrift. I shared with her the basic principles of contemplative prayer and Lectio Devina. Recognizing that her family situation was very tenuous and fragile, she immediately put it into practice.

After a couple of months there was a noticeable change in her life, and she felt more calm and positive. Often it was hard to find time to pray, especially with two young children, but she persevered. An on-going relationship with God, though at times involving intense struggle, is often associated with increased courage, perseverance, and peace. Jesus said that we should always pray and not be overwhelmed. "For the eyes of the Lord are on the righteous and his ears are attentive to their prayer" (1 Peter 3:12). Through prayer this dear lady was able to glimpse God's presence in her situation, giving her courage and hope.

Two changed lives

A great friend, Donald Wheeler, was searching for ways to gain more focus in his Christian life as he felt "broken, exhausted and out of focus." He began to practice contemplative prayer after listening to audiotapes by Father Thomas Keating. It became his practice, twice a day, to spend twenty minutes in the silence of contemplative prayer. In preparation he would take a few minutes for worship, using a daily lectionary, very specific intercessory prayers, and a preparatory exercise that included attention to breathing. He recalls,

> The racing thoughts gradually slow down, helped by my
> gently returning to a sacred word. Maybe there are only a
> few seconds during the twenty minutes when there are no
> thoughts, just peace. As the end approaches I ease my
> way back to ordinary consciousness, pray the Lord's
> prayer and ask a blessing for all God's creation. Often
> then I will consider what lies ahead in the day. Much of
> the stress and anxiety will have disappeared. I feel
> liberated rather than driven. I feel free to drop things
> from my 'to do' list that now seem unnecessary. Some
> important priority may rise up to replace them. And my
> mind—probably with a better balance of left brain and
> right brain activity—goes to work to find a way to move
> forward. I find myself more able to face the difficult tasks
> ahead. I feel God will guide and strengthen me no matter
> what the day brings.

After following this discipline for four years, he said that it had become his most important individual spiritual practice, providing an inner peace that lasted the whole day through. Although no two times of contemplation were exactly the same, he never felt that his time could have been better spent. When rushing and late, he would sometimes take a few minutes for contemplation to "give God a chance to straighten me out." When battling with his ego, he no longer felt the need to beat up on himself, but simply allowed God to "be my Abba again" in silence. The eternal perspective also encouraged him to take better care of his body, exercising and eating more healthily. For this man contemplative prayer was life changing.

Another very poignant example concerns a brilliant lawyer who was a member of a major firm. He was very tense, rushed, somewhat obsessive, always distracted, and extremely controlling. He had become frustrated with his church, feeling somehow that he would go Sunday after Sunday in an autonomous way, but leave feeling empty, rejected, and unfulfilled. I shared with him the practice of contemplative prayer and Lectio Devina and he became extremely interested, making his own study, which led him to a number of silent retreats and to Father Keating and Snowmass Mountain, Colorado. I noticed in this gentleman, in a matter of months, a total change of personality. He became calm, likeable, pleasant, and had time to be with people. It is my conviction that prayer does change things.

CONCLUSION

I realize that Lectio Devina and contemplative prayer are not for everyone. For some people the silence may be very difficult, and they would find simply reading scripture with verbal prayer more helpful. But I would like to encourage you, even if you feel that this is not your particular prayer method, to open yourselves to scripture. Just by meditating on scripture God may lead us into silence and open to us the grace of contemplation. Christ taught his disciples that they should always pray and not give up (Luke 18:1-8). It seems that we have two choices in life. Either to pray or to give up. But the most important dynamic of contemplative prayer is that it leads us to the shedding of our false selves and their empty illusions and attachments. It opens us up to our true selves in God.

REFERENCES

1. Andrew Louth, *The Origins of the Christian Mystical Tradition* (Oxford: Oxford University Press, Clarendon Paperbacks, 1981).
2. David Allen Jr, (unpublished).
3. *The Cloud of Unknowing,* trans. William Johnson (Garden City, New York: Doubleday, 1973).
4. Thomas Merton, quoted by William Shannon in *Seeds of Peace* (New York: Crossword, 1996). 55.

5. Thomas Merton, *Seeds of Contemplation* (New York: New Directions, 1949).

6. Henri J. M. Nouwen, *Out of Solitude*, (Notre Dame, Indiana: Ava Maria Press, 1974).

7. Victor Franco, *Psychotherapy of Existentialism* (New York: Simon and Schuster, 1967).

8. Joseph Chu-Cong, *The Contemplative Experience* (New York: Crossword, 1999).

9. St Francis, quoted in Joseph Chu-Cong, *The Contemplative Experience* (New York: Crossword, 1999), 3.

10. St. Bernard of Clairvaux, quoted in Joseph Chu-Cong, *The Contemplative Experience* (New York: Crossword, 1999), 3.

11. William Shakespeare, *As You Like It,* Act one, Scene two.

12. Gerard Manley Hopkins, "God's Grandeur" in *The Oxford Book of English Mystical Verse,* ed Nicholson and Lee (Oxford: Clarendon Press, 1917).

13. D.T. Suzuki, quoted by Joseph Chu-Cong in *The Contemplative Experience* (New York: Crossword, 1999), 4.

14. Joseph Chu-Cong, *The Contemplative Experience* (New York: Crossword, 1999), 4.

15. St. John Climacus, quoted by Joseph Chu-Cong in *The Contemplative Experience* (New York: Crossword, 1999), 4.

16. T.S. Eliot, *The Waste Land* (New York: Boni and Liveright, 1922).

17. Joseph Chu-Cong, *The Contemplative Experience* (New York: Crossword, 1999), 39.

18. Elizabeth Barrett Browning, "Aurora Leigh" in *Aurora Leigh and Other Poems,* ed John Robert Glorney Bolton and Julia Bolton Holloway (Harmondsworth: Penguin, 1995).

19. Henri J. M. Nouwen, *The Return of the Prodigal Son: A Story of Homecoming* (New York: Doubleday, 1992).

20. William H. Shannon, *Seeds of Peace* (New York: Crossword, 1996), 14.

21. *The Cloud of Unknowing,* trans. William Johnson (Garden City, New York: Doubleday, 1973), 9-10.

22. Scott Peck, *The Road Less Travelled* (New York: Simon and Schuster, 1978).

23. T.S. Elliot, "The Journey of the Magi," in *Collected Poems* 1909-1962 (New York: Harcourt, 1963).

CHAPTER 6
THE TRUE SELF: AUTHENTIC REALITY

Life batters and shapes us in all sort of ways before it is done...The original, shim-
mering self gets buried so deep that most of us hardly end up living out of it at all.
Instead, we live out of all the other selves which we are constantly putting on and
taking off like coats and hats against the world's weather. (Frederick Buechner[1])

Zacchaeus, a short little man, wielded tremendous power because of his
infamous reputation as a harsh, cruel tax collector for the occupying
Romans. Zacchaeus not only collected the taxes people owed, he would
add extra taxes, sometimes even quadrupling the amount collected; he
was hated, dreaded, and feared by the people (Luke 19:1-10).

Hearing that Jesus, the well-known rabbi whose miracles were the talk
of the district, was passing through his town, Zacchaeus yearned to meet
him. He was wealthy, but not a contented man. I think he was probably
hurt in childhood—he may have felt abandoned, inadequately loved, rejected. He may have been punished severely by his superiors, and so would
have been constantly defending against a powerful sense of shame.
Compensating through his false self, he sought security by obtaining exces-
sive money in corrupt ways; afraid of rejection, he became totally self-

absorbed and lived by the rule of *all for me baby.* People feared him and so he became powerful and manipulative. But all this was not enough to satisfy the deepest longings of his heart. Yearning for something more, Zacchaeus wanted to meet Jesus.

Zacchaeus was unable to see over the heads of the crowd because he was short. The people who blocked his view hated him, so he set his dignity aside and climbed up a sycamore tree to catch a view of Jesus. As Jesus was passing by he looked up and commanded an amazed Zacchaeus to come down. Seeing a needy individual rather than a despised collaborator, Jesus told Zacchaeus he would come to his home and spend some time with his family. Zacchaeus was touched and surprised by Jesus' interest in him; it made him feel loved and cared for. We can only imagine the shock and confusion of the crowd at Jesus' desire to spend time with this horrible person. Throughout the gospel Jesus was always easier on overt expressions of wrongdoing than on hypocritical, self-righteous attitudes.

Going to Zacchaeus' home, Jesus spent time with him and his family, and they shared a meal. Deeply moved and loved, Zacchaeus dropped his defensive false self and opened to his inner wounded self. Continuing to be loved, Zacchaeus opened to his true self in God, and with his family came to new understanding of contemplation—the vision of God and the mission of God's love in the world. The experience of contemplation is always transforming, and Zacchaeus made a commitment to right the wrongs he had done. In an act of repentance he promised to pay back fourfold the people he had cheated. This simple but profound story illustrates the discovery of the true self, whose identity is based on the unchanging, unconditional love of God.

DEFINING THE TRUE SELF

Henri Nouwen tells the story of a sculptor, working hard with his hammer and chisel on a large block of marble. A little boy, who had no idea what the sculptor was doing, was watching him. When the boy returned to the studio a few weeks later he saw, to his great surprise, a large, powerful lion sitting in the place where the marble has stood. Very excited the boy ran to the sculptor, "Sir, tell me, how did you know that there was a lion in the marble?" the sculptor replied, "I knew because before I saw the lion in the marble, I saw the lion in my heart."

As Henri Nouwen observed, "The art of sculpture is first of all the art of seeing. In one block of marble, Michelangelo saw a loving mother with a dead son on her lap; in another, he saw a self-confident David ready to hurl a stone at the approaching Goliath; and in a third, he saw Moses at the point of rising in anger from his seat."[2] In contemplation, God the sculptor chips away the marble of our false selves to reveal our true selves in him.

The deepest part of our lives, the true self, represents our identity— that we are created in the image of God. This awareness of our authentic self in God's love, in order to become a functional reality, must be nurtured and developed by the unconditional acceptance of God's presence and action in our lives. But life is wounded and as Frederick Buechner so poignantly states,

> The original, shimmering self gets buried so deep that
> most of us hardly end up living out of it at all. Instead,
> we live out of all the other selves which we are constantly
> putting on and taking off like coats and hats against the
> world's weather.[3]

Being authentic in this world is not easy. Pulled this way and that by different demands, we have little time to think about who we are, why we are here, and where we are going. As a result, we become blind to our deeper, true selves and end up living sometimes 40 to 60 percent below our God-given potential. The true self, unlike the false self, does not define our identity by what we do, how useful we are, what we have, or how well we are thought of, but as a person beloved by God. God loves us with a love that will never let us go and a face that will never turn away. Created in the image of God, we are spiritual beings seeking to make sense of our human existence.

AWARENESS OF THE TRUE SELF

Our lives are like the sea: one day a flat calm and the next a raging storm. Below the waves, deep in the water, it is calm and still, representing our sense of being. The seabed is solid and unmoving, representing the unchanging God in whose image we are made. In contemplative prayer, as we allow ourselves to become impregnated by the naked love of the unchanging Eternal Being, our false selves melt away revealing our true selves, our essential beings. We are still pushed to and fro by the waves of our daily lives, but no longer tossed about because our feet are firmly planted on the solid seabed below. God's grace is always available if we continually seek it and receive it by faith. We still have moments of turmoil, but as we allow God's grace to impact on our changing and unpredictable life situations, we can choose to live in the awareness that all is well with our souls.

The temptation of modern culture is to confuse our life situations with the essence of our lives: when things are good, life is good; when things are bad, life is bad. Thus our very sense of being becomes precarious and superficial. Because we are created in the image of God, our deepest desire is to see the face of God, and as we reach out to him he anchors our lives anew. As St. Augustine said so many years ago, "We shall ever restless be until we find our rest in thee."[4]

Appreciating the identity of our true selves requires an awareness of its reality. If we stop to think about it, to define ourselves by what we do, by what we possess, or by how people see us, is laughable. We do not have to perform in order to be. We simply are. But this is so difficult to grasp in the modern Western culture that surrounds us. The advertising media, one of the most powerful gods of our day, promotes and encourages a powerful consumerism, which tends to define us and encourage the development of our false selves. The sad reality is that we are all affected, making it difficult to free ourselves from the constructs of the false self. The true self is somewhat intangible and it is something we must experience rather than explain. Once we become aware of our deeper or true selves in God—the ground of our being—we experience a transformation of consciousness based on love. Instead of depending on our false selves for our identity, we come to recognize that our being flows from the divine creative energy, from the great *I am*.

Our *I* can never be characterized: I am rich, I am poor, I am educated, I am uneducated, but I am still the same person. The essential person is the same because we are made in the image of the Eternal Being. Reality allows us to face life with courage, hope, and love, recognizing that "if God is for us, who can be against us?" (Romans 8:31). Although we may not have what we want, we may not have achieved our goals; we are still defined by God's love that gives us new meaning and purpose in both temporal and eternal perspectives. According to Basil Pennington,

> Certainly once I know that I am ever embraced by the divine creative love, loved by love itself, by the love that is a source of all there is, then I certainly will never again see myself created by what others think. If I am any longer concerned by what others think, it is only because I want our relationship to exist in the domain of truth, to be what it truly is and not based on phoniness.[5]

FRUITS OF LIVING IN THE TRUE SELF

Our true selves, created in the image of God, are associated with love, joy, and peace. Described as the fruits of God living in us, they relate to God himself, our relationships with others, and of course our relationship to ourselves. This divine love, joy, and peace are not conditional, ordinary, mundane values or emotions but are constant states of being. The love of God is unchanging. The peace of God exists beyond understanding and conflict. The joy of God ever flows in both pain and pleasure, good times and bad times. That which is most personal is also most universal. As I open up to my true self in God I touch other human beings as well. My life is like a bicycle wheel, with God at the center, the hub. When I live in my false self, off-center, then I am not connected to all the spokes. When I move to the hub, my true self in God, then God's love radiates like spokes to the whole rim, touching all parts of my life. The test of our true selves in God is validated by the experience of deeper relationships, a sense of oneness with all other people. Our relationships with each other will be characterized by a sense of patience—that is learning to suffer with others and feel their pain, and a sense of kindness—learning to show mercy and be forgiving. At its deepest level the true self also has important personal qualities such as faithfulness, humility, and self-control. Faithfulness, in both the big and small things of life, means learning to accept the goodness of life, recognizing that good overcomes evil and love overcomes hate. Humility or gentleness means recognizing our limitations and our place in the universe, recognizing that life is mystery and that there is much we don't know. Humility means making an honest assessment of ourselves in the presence of God and each other. Self-control does not mean perfection, but the desire to move towards maturity in love. This is not a magical transformation, but the true self, when awakened, creates a desire for growth and development in all aspects of our being.

COMMUNITY AND THE TRUE SELF

The concept of the true self in God produces a sense of oneness with Christ, with our common humanity, and with the environment. We experience the mystery of God's love working in each other and creating a community where we love our neighbors as our own x-rayed selves. The experience of the true self is not a quick fix, but a maturation that takes place over time. It is a gift of God. In contemplative prayer there is an active perspective, where we are involved in the practice of prayer, and then there is passive acceptance, which is the gift of God. In other words, as we open ourselves through our regular practice of prayer, we wait on God to reveal the essence of himself by his love, faithfulness, and joy. These are gifts; they cannot be demanded or negotiated. Learning to wait, our job is to continue praying and leave the outcome to God.

The true self allows us to experience the meaning of solitude, a time of being alone with the Alone. Unless we can be alone with God and ourselves, we have very little to offer others; solitude allows us to establish community or communion with others. Without solitude we experience loneliness and loneliness in the presence of others produces a crowd. Thus, opening ourselves to love in our true selves in God, we experience the real meaning of communion and community.

THE TRUE SELF IN THE IMAGE OF GOD

As we perceive more clearly our true selves in God, we are all but dazzled by the wonder of being made in the image of God. We are profoundly humbled to realize that, although life is wounded and the image is often badly scarred, the image and likeness of God are there. Facing the true self means coming to accept our identity as a person loved by God. This is easier said than done; it is difficult to break through the powerful false-self reality of seeing our lives as dependent on what we possess, what we do, or what others think of us. Recognizing that we are persons beloved of

God is accepting our lives regardless of whether we are sick or well, rich or poor, because God's loving grace allows us to be in him. This is the sunshine piercing the darkness of our lives. According to Merton,

> The experience of contemplation is the experience of God's life and presence within ourselves not as object, but as the transcendent source of our own subjectivity. Contemplation is mystery in which God reveals himself to us as the very center of our own most intimate self. [6]

In the revelation of God's presence, the false self is destroyed and we experience our true selves. According to Paul, "I have been crucified with Christ [meaning my false self]; and I no longer live, but Christ lives in me [my true self]" (Galatians 2:20). In a deep sense the true self is God living in us, rejuvenating our being by his divine energy. DeMello reminds us that when we awaken to our true selves it is painful to see our illusions shattered and everything we built up crumble.[7] This is the repentance that changes our life.

THE TRUE SELF AND SEEING

In our everyday world, as we get older we internalize images of various external objects. When a child is with a hibiscus flower they are actually seeing the flower—they do not already have an internalized image of the flower. But as the child grows older, the awareness of the external image of the flower is counteracted by their internal image of the flower. In time they become so addicted to the internalized image of the flower in their head that they miss the external reality of being with the flower. Being our true selves is becoming present with the real flower again; learning to feel its petals, appreciate its colors, and smell its aroma, to be with it. Grasped by the beauty of the flower, we realize that we both originate from the same source—the love that will never let us go and the face that never turns away. Instilling a child-like curiosity, this awareness gives us courage and allows us to see the beauty of life. The false self, on the other hand, sees life with a mundane mediocrity. It sees life as boring and repetitive, leaving us untouched and uninspired. If we allow ourselves to break the addiction to our internalized images, we will once again see clearly. As William Blake writes, "When the doors of perception are cleansed, man will see things as they truly are, infinite." [8] To understand that God is constantly reaching out to us in love is heart warming. He always comes. He comes in the thunder. He comes in the rain. He comes through people. He comes through circumstances. But he always comes to share his love, to share his peace, to share his joy. There will always be resistance, something to block our awareness of God's love. At the last supper, when Jesus was sharing intimate fellowship with his disciples, there was Judas, planning to destroy the whole thing. But Jesus did not let this interfere with God's program. He still broke bread, took the cup and gave it to his disciples. He still washed the disciples' feet—even the feet of Judas. Evil will always be present, but it does not have the power to block God's love and presence.

THE TRUE SELF AND UNLOADING THE UNCONSCIOUS

The human heart cries out for safety. When people feel safe they share their pain, let go of their anger, and give up their resentments. Contemplative prayer opens us to the presence and action of the eternal God in our lives. As a result we experience a sense of safety and relaxation, allowing our hearts to release the hurts and pain embedded in our bodies. Contemplative prayer makes us safe as we open to the presence of the eternal God, "if God is for us, who can be against us?" (Romans 8:31). As we relax or rest in his presence, our bodies and minds release or unload the hurts and wounds of a lifetime. Unlike psychotherapy, there may not be any verbal expression but the general release of pain can take the form of a grunt, a murmur, a tremor, or sometimes a sense of sadness and grief during and after the time of prayer. Our childhood trauma is embedded not only in our hearts but also all through our bodies. And so, as we remain still before God and open ourselves to the rhythm of his love, his healing grace releases the hurts of a lifetime. Contemplative prayer, according to Father Keating, is "divine therapy".[9] The surgeon may cut, the physician may prescribe, the preacher may preach, but only God's love heals. The Psalmist said long ago,

When I said, 'My foot is slipping,'
your love, O Lord, supported me.

When anxiety was great within me,
your consolation brought joy to my soul (Psalm 94:18-19).

God is the one who comforts us in times of conflict, trouble, and difficult issues. "My soul finds rest in God alone" (Psalms 62:1). We never fully live out the true self in this life. Life is wounded and we have feelings of abandonment, rejection, and shame; so we will always seek the defenses of our false selves. Nevertheless, our task is to do the grief work of our early childhood-hurt by breaking up the unplowed ground of our hearts to release our hurt and pain and experience the freedom of our true selves in God. "In him we live and move and have our being" (Acts 17:28). Christ said it another way, "Remain in me, and I will remain in you" (John 15:4). David said, "You prepare a table before me in the presence of my enemies" (Psalm 23:5) As we enter contemplative prayer the external silence gives rise to an internal silence, which then creates a powerful stillness, leading to an interior space, a place where we can be with God at the table set for two. He brings us his banqueting feast of love and, in spite of the pain and ups and downs of life, he gives us a joy, he gives us courage, he gives us hope (Song of Songs 7:12-13).

THE TRUE SELF AND THE ORDINARY

The true self encounters God in the ordinary things of life. Living in our true selves means becoming truly present. So often the false self causes us to live in a past-future prison—we dwell on the past, which projects pictures to the future, and we completely miss the present. Remember everything happens in the present and when we miss the present, we also miss the Presence of God himself. I am reminded of my friend Henry Nouwen, who wrote so clearly to a New York intellectual,

All I want to say to you is this, you are the beloved, and all I hope is that you can hear these words as spoken to you with all the tenderness and force that life can hold. My only desire is to make these words reverberate in every corner of your being, you are the beloved. [10]

As we open to our true selves in God through contemplation, the vision of God inspires us to seek the mission of God's love in the world. As a result life is no longer a series of disconnected events but a window into the love of God. According to Nouwen, the movement from opaqueness to transparency occurs in three central relationships—nature, time, and people.

Nature

In contemplation nature is not a property to be possessed but a gift to be received with amazement and gratitude. For example, if we see a tree as nothing but a potential chair, it has little to say to us. As part of God's creation, it has much to say.

Time

Linear time experienced as *chronos* becomes opaque leading to fatalism and boredom. Boredom does not mean we have nothing to do or insufficient entertainment, it is rather the horrible feeling that what we do makes no real difference. Contemplation opens us up to our true selves, which see time as *kairos* (God's time) the fullness of time or timelessness, so that all the events of our lives lead to meaning and fulfillment. As a result, daily tasks like writing letters, cooking, and serving become transformative possibilities for renewal and change.

People

In our true selves, we see people as part of our relationship with God, a fascinating unity in the midst of diversity. Derived from the Latin roots *per* and *sonare*, a person is a *sounding through*. Hence our gift to others is to reveal to them that they sound through or reveal a greater love than they know, a deeper truth than they understand, and a more magnificent beauty than they can contain.[11]

LIFE IN SILENCE

This sense of being loved is directly related to opening up to the prayer of silence. Silence is not just the absence of noise or the shutting down of communication with the outside world, but rather a process of coming to stillness. It is learning to be still and know the presence of God. Healing words come from silence, are accompanied by silence, and return to silence. And so silence and solitude forge true and meaningful speech. Solitude does not mean physical isolation. Solitude means being alone with the Alone, experiencing the transcendent other, and growing in awareness of our identity as the beloved. I believe that it is impossible to know another person intimately without first spending time with ourselves. Silence provides that opportunity for solitude with God and ourselves. True silence always creates interior silence and interior silence always creates space: space for God, for ourselves, and for others. True solitude opens the door to the development of meaningful community. Without solitude we have isolation or loneliness and instead of creating community we create a crowd. Contemplative prayer is a process of opening to our true selves and creating a meaningful solitude and community, but outside of our prayer time, influenced by the small things that pull and tear at us, we so easily forget that we are the beloved.

There is a beautiful description of the importance of silence in the story of an executive who went to see a hermit for advice. The hermit listened closely to the man's story of struggle and conflict and of his inability to lead a truly spiritual life. After a while the hermit went into the dark recesses of his cave and came out with a basin and a pitcher of water. He then asked the man to watch the water as he poured it into the basin. The water splashed on the bottom and against the sides of the container, it was agitated and turbulent. It swirled around the inside of the basin and then gradually began to settle until there were only gentle swells that oscillated back and forth. Eventually the surface of the water became so smooth that the executive could see his face reflected. The hermit said gently, "It takes time for the water to settle just like it takes time to come to stillness. Coming to interior stillness and interior silence requires waiting, patience, and time. Any attempt to hasten the process only stirs the water anew." [12]

The agitated water is our lives when we are constantly in the midst of others. We cannot see ourselves as we really are because of all the confusion and disturbance, we fail to recognize the divine presence in our lives and the consciousness of being beloved slowly fades. Learning to understand the true self means coming to grips with the importance of patience, the importance of waiting, the importance of being alone, and the importance of being silent. But most of all it means recognizing that the gift of stillness comes from God himself. It is our job to be faithful in our practice of contemplative prayer, but it is up to God to give us the gift of stillness, the gift of himself. He has promised that those who seek him will find him, and to those who knock, the door will be opened.

LISTENING

There are three levels of listening: phenomenal (surface), existential (problem solving), and contemplative (communion). So often in our rushed lives we stay at the phenomenal level just listening on the surface, or maybe even at the existential level when we try to problem solve. But to understand the deeper levels of life, we have to reach the contemplative level. It's a place where we are required to wait patiently and listen in silence. It means listening another person into being. If I am not in touch with my own belovedness then I cannot touch the sacredness of others. If I am a stranger to myself, I am likewise a stranger to others. The fact is, we connect best with others when we connect with the core of ourselves. As we connect to the core of ourselves we touch the ground of our being that is God himself. As Manning says,

> When I allow God to liberate me from unhealthy dependence on people, I listen more attentively, love more unselfishly, and I am more compassionate and playful. I take myself less seriously, become aware that the breath of the Father is on my face and that my countenance is bright with laughter and a mystical adventure I thoroughly enjoy. [13]

Spending time in silent or contemplative prayer allows God to speak and act with greater strength in our lives. It gives us the freedom to forgive rather than to nurse the latest bruises of our wounded egos, it allows us to be capable of magnanimity during the petty moments of life; it empowers us to have courage despite the background tableaux of our fears and insecurities. Many times when we practice deep, silent prayer we become sleepless, but at the same time more energetic. It seems to me that the huge amount of energy expended by our false selves in the pursuit of illusory happiness is now available to be focused on the things that really matter: love, friendship, and intimacy with God. Contemplation allows us to recognize that knowing God is living with the real and all that is real. We hear him speak to us, we hear him say in a very quiet but affirming way, "Fear not, for I have redeemed you; I have summoned you by name; you are mine...you are precious and honored in my sight," (Isaiah 43:1,4) and "Though the mountains be shaken and the hills be removed, yet my unfailing love for you will not be shaken nor my covenant of peace be removed" (Isaiah 54:10).

THE TRUE SELF AND THE MYSTERY OF GOD

As we grasp the understanding of what it means to be present with God and open to our true selves in him, we experience the mystery of God's presence. So often we speak glibly of knowing God, but it is very important for us to remember that great is the mystery of Godliness (I Timothy 3:16). In a sense we are hushed and trembling. We are creatures in the presence of an ethical mystery that is above all and beyond all telling. The apostle, speaking of our relationship in God says, "This is a profound mystery" (Ephesians 5:32), and "the mystery that has been kept hidden for ages and generations, but is now disclosed to the saints" (Colossians 1:26). No wonder the prophet Isaiah exclaims, "Holy, holy, holy is the Lord Almighty, the whole earth is full of his glory" (Isaiah 6:3). Coming to grips with our true selves in God is a journey; it doesn't mean we have arrived. It is a struggle to be constantly aware of our core identity—that we are the beloved of God. It requires a steadfast commitment not to be influenced by peers who spend their lives courting applause and admiration. As Jesus said, we are to be in the world, but not of the world (John 17:14-15).

According to DeMello, "coming to grips with the inner reality of our true self in God is possible even though we are bogged down with issues relating to our false self,"[14] that is, being defined by what we do, possess, or how people think about us. Being our true selves involves paying attention to our experience of life and learning to listen attentively as the God who loves us speaks to us through the ordinary circumstances of our lives. As our identity is in being loved by God, God the lover is always moving towards us, the beloved. As mentioned earlier in this chapter, God always comes. He comes in the rain, in the sunshine, through the sea, through the land, through the mountains, the damns, or the beautiful woods. This is not to say that there is no suffering and pain in our world; slavery, the Holocaust, brutal dictatorships and social injustice all bare witness to dreadful suffering and pain. But Christians throughout the centuries have experienced God's presence in the midst of persecution and suffering. They persevered by faith as indicated in Hebrews 11:27 "He [Moses] persevered because he saw him who is invisible." In contemplative prayer, as we develop a deeper awareness of the presence of God in our lives, then we too may endure by seeing "him who is invisible."

God comes through people, he comes through situations, he comes through our so-called successes, but he also comes through negative situations, through our failures and addictions. He always comes because he loves us. Because we are the beloved we can never be alone. The one who loves us is always with us. From a psychological point of view we can open to the true self by eliminating our defenses through a good supportive, therapeutic, understanding environment. However, the true self finds its basic security in the awareness of the presence of God in our lives, and for us as Christians it is through the risen presence of the Lord Jesus Christ, " Since, then, you have been raised with Christ, set your hearts on things above" (Colossians 3:1). It calls for us to move beyond the false self and open to the risen Christ in every aspect of our lives. As we open to our true selves in God we experience a clarity and a purity, "Blessed are the pure in heart, for they will see God" (Matthew 5:8). This does not mean that we are perfect, or have no woundedness, or are without sin, but it does mean an increased sensitivity to please and serve God. Whenever we fail or refuse to do good as the opportunity arises, in some sense we are not just missing the mark, our true selves are repressed and we open to our false selves.

Brennan Manning tells a very poignant story about a Jewish couple who had married with great love and commitment. They hoped to have a child to share their love; eventually their prayers were answered and Mordecai was born. He grew to be a rambunctious, energetic child. The sun and moon were his toys. He grew in age, wisdom, and grace until it was time for him to go to the synagogue to learn the word of God. According to Manning, the night before Mordecai's studies began his parents sat him down and told him how important it was to learn the word of

God. They told him that without the word of God his life would be like an autumn leaf blowing in the wind. But Mordecai felt very self-sufficient, he didn't feel the need for God. Instead of going to the synagogue he went to the woods to swim in the lake and climb the trees. We are sometimes very like Mordecai. The news quickly spread throughout the village, embarrassing the parents who became very, very angry. They sought help from the local therapist but to no avail. The next day Mordecai once again returned to the woods to swim in the lake and climb the trees. His parents called in all the elders and healers for advice, but to no avail; Mordecai again went to the woods to swim in the lake and climb the trees. Upset and grieved for their beloved son, the parents felt hopeless.

One day a great rabbi visited the village and the parents asked him to please help their son. Calling Mordecai to himself, the rabbi picked him up and held him silently against his heart. As the two hearts felt each other beating together this had a profound effect on Mordecai, who became aware for the first time of how much he was loved. The next day he went straight to the synagogue to learn the word of God, and when he was done he went back to the woods. But somehow in the woods the word of God became one with the word of the woods which became one with the words of Mordecai. And as he swam in the lake, the word of God became one with the word of the lake which became one with the word of Mordecai and as he climbed the trees the word of God became one with the words of the trees which became one with the word of Mordecai. Eventually Mordecai himself grew up and became a great man. People seized with panic and many hurts came to him and found help and peace. People who were lonely, frustrated, and isolated in life came to him and found communion. People who were trapped came to him and found a way out. When Mordecai was asked what his secret was he said, "I first learnt the word of God when the great rabbi held me silently against his heart."[15] And so in our lives it is only when we accept ourselves as being loved by God, when we realize that we are held next to the heart of God, that our false selves melt away and open us up to our true selves and open our eyes and ears to the word of God in scripture, nature, our daily situations, and in each other.

IMMACULATA'S STORY

A few years ago, when I was giving a lecture on drug addiction in Prague at the famous old University of Charles, a very attractive nun walked in, who radiated with an aura. At the end of my lecture I went to inquire who she was, and she told me a moving story. She said her father had been a very active Christian who was tortured and killed by the communist government because of his beliefs. After this she decided to become the worst young girl in Prague so that people, particularly the teachers, would know that she was not a believer like her dad. Using drugs, practicing prostitution, she did everything conceivably evil to prove that she was a bad girl. In other words, she opened to her false self to defend against her pain, the pain of her loss at the death of her father.

Then one night, while attending a rock concert in Slovakia with some friends, the roof fell in and she was hurt. But, because she was high on drugs, her friends were afraid to go to the hospital for help, and she found herself in an old broken-down house in the woods, her chest hurting deeply. She was terrified and cried profusely. Remembering her father she cried and felt so alone. Then she noticed a crucifix on the wall in the dilapidated old house. She said, "One day, Dr. Allen, I heard the crucifix saying, 'Why are you running from me? I love you, I have always been with you, you belong to me, you are mine.'" With tears in her eyes, even though she was still in pain, she opened her heart and said, "Lord Jesus, I give my life to you, I am no longer ashamed of my father's faith. Regardless of what happens I want to give my life to you. I want to follow you." When she recovered she went to a convent and told them that she wanted to serve God with her life. Entering the convent as a novice, her name was changed to Immaculata, which means without sin. She heard that I was lecturing on drug treatment and came to learn more about drugs because now her mission is to work the streets of Prague helping young boys and girls to stay off drugs and getting help for those who are addicted. As I sat with this beautiful person I realized that she had described the transformation of the false self into the true self in God. In fact I felt that I was in the very presence of God himself, Immaculata, Immaculata, Immaculata.

CONCLUSION

In the early part of the chapter, the little boy asked the sculptor how he knew there was a lion in the marble. This question becomes for us, how do we know there is a God in the world? The answer of the sculptor is simple, but profound, "I knew there was a lion in the marble because, before I saw the lion in the marble I saw him in my heart." [16] God the sculptor sees our true selves because we are made in his image. And so, in contemplation, God within us recognizes God in the world. "For God so loved the world that he gave his one and only Son, that whoever believes in him shall not perish but have eternal life" (John 3:16).

"Unless a grain of wheat falls to the ground and dies, it remains only a single seed" (John 12:24). But if it is planted, watered, and fertilized, the hard outer shell falls away, the seed comes to life and it bears much fruit. If we allow ourselves to be nurtured in contemplation by the deep love of God, our defensive false selves, developed to protect us from our childhood traumas, melt away and allow our true selves in God to flourish.

REFERENCES

1. Frederick Buechner, *Telling Secrets* (San Francisco: Harper, 1991), 44-45.

2. Henri J. M. Nouwen, *Clowning in Rome: Reflections on Solitude, Celibacy, Prayer, and Contemplation* (Garden City, New York: Doubleday, 1979), 87.

3. Frederick Buechner, *Telling Secrets* (San Francisco: Harper, 1991), 45.

4. St. Augustine of Hippo, *Confessions of St. Augustine,* trans. John Ryan, (New York: Image Books, 1960).

5. Basil M. Pennington, *True Self / False Self: Unmasking the Spirit Within* (New York: Crossroad, 2000).

6. Thomas Merton, *The New Man* (New York: Farrar, Straus and Cudahy, 1961), 19.

7. Anthony DeMello, *Awareness* (Garden City, New York: Doubleday, 1991), 45.

8. William Blake, "The Marriage of Heaven and Hell".

9. Thomas Keating, *Open Mind Open Heart* (New York: Continuum, 1999), 13.

10. Henri J. M. Nouwen, *The Life of the Beloved,* (New York: Crossword,

1992), 30.

11. Henri J. M. Nouwen, *Clowning in Rome: Reflections on Solitude, Celibacy, Prayer, and Contemplation* (Garden City, New York: Doubleday, 1979), 92-95.

12. Brennan Manning, *Abba's Child: The cry of the Heart for Intimate Belonging* (Colorado Springs, Colorado: Navpress, 1994), 57.

13. Brennan Manning, *Abba's Child: The cry of the Heart for Intimate Belonging* (Colorado Springs, Colorado: Navpress, 1994), p58

14. Anthony DeMello, *Awareness* (Garden City, New York: Doubleday, 1991), 45.

15. Brennan Manning, *Abba's Child: The cry of the Heart for Intimate Belonging* (Colorado Springs, Colorado: Navpress, 1994), 119-121.

16. Henri J. M. Nouwen, *Clowning in Rome: Reflections on Solitude, Celibacy, Prayer, and Contemplation* (Garden City, New York: Doubleday, 1979), 87.

Part Two: Contemplation In the Lives of God's People

CHAPTER 7
ABRAHAM: THE SOUL'S JOURNEY TO GOD

The message of Abraham is to be alone, to be quiet, and to listen. If you never hear the Call in the first place, you'll never know which way to go. (Father John[1])

Abraham, the patriarch of three of the world's leading religions—Judaism, Christianity, and Islam—is a pivotal person in human historya. It is fitting that we should look at his life because of his fundamental role in the formation of the human religious psyche. Reflected in his life we see much of our own lives. According to Feiler, "This Abraham is not a Jew, Christian or Muslim. He is not flawless; he is not a saint. But he is himself, the best vessel we've got, the father of all."[3]

    Raised in the ancient civilization of Ur in the Chaldees where the moon god Nana was worshipped, Abraham was called by God to leave his home country and journey to the land of Canaan, the Promised Land. God always initiates the Call to know him more, because he is deeper and higher than all we could ever be. As God called Abraham, he also calls us to seek him in faith. Faith is a gift from God, validating his love and allowing trust to develop. Faith colors all aspects of our lives with meaning, purpose and grace. Like his call to us, the call of God to Abraham was comprehensive. God asked Abraham to leave his background, his family, and his community. Leaving is always difficult. It is so hard for human beings to say goodbye. The call of faith is a spiritual journey asking us to say goodbye to our present lifestyle, our likes and dislikes, our friends and our enemies.

God's call to Abraham was clear, but Abraham found it difficult to leave because of his father, Terah, who challenged Abraham not to go all the way to Canaan but instead to go to Haran, which means halfway or half-baked, or parched. So often Haran represents our spiritual journey; we sacrifice the call of God on our lives to please our parents or peers, to bow to our addictions and lifestyles. With this half-baked devotional spirituality, we invite God into our hearts as the guest, but we ourselves still seek to lead the dance and call the shots, and in the words of Frank Sinatra's famous song, "I did it my way." In contemplative spirituality, on the other hand, although we first invite God as the guest, we then bow to him and allow him to become the host and guide of our lives. Our goal is not what we want, but what God calls us to, in spite of the difficulties involved. In other words, when God calls us to Canaan, instead of just going part of the way to Haran—instead of having a half-baked faith—we go all the way. Lord, not my will but your will be done (Matthew 26:42).

Faith in our modern world is often just this: half-baked or incomplete. It was not until Abraham's father died that he followed his call into Canaan. It may be helpful at this time to ask ourselves, in the quietness and sacredness of our souls, what is holding us back from moving on in our spiritual journeys? Is it relationships? Is it family? Is it material possessions? Is it some negative habit? Is it a sense of failure? Or do we just feel unworthy to be on the spiritual journey?

ALTARS AND TENTS

Arriving in Canaan, Abraham built an altar to worship God and pitched a tent (Genesis 12:8). The altar and the tent are both characteristic of a spiritual journey. The altar represents our commitment to giving God the supreme place in our lives. The altar is the place where we meet God, the place where we call upon God, the place where we respond to the call of God. The tent reminds us that life is transitory and that we are on a journey. Whenever we replace God on the altar of our lives, we create idols or addictions. Whenever we replace the tent we forget that life is transitory and create a mausoleum, a kind of death in the midst of life. It may be a beautiful home or a great business but without the context of the altar and the recognition of the tent, it is death in the midst of life. Knowing God or moving into a deeper spirituality, which I define as contemplation, involves respecting God on the altar of our lives and remembering that we live in a tent.

After Abraham established his altar and pitched his tent, we might expect all to be well. In our spiritual journeys we often expect to arrive at a place where we will be at peace and all will be well. However, the spiritual journey is a relationship, a relationship with a God who never promised us a bed of roses, that things would be easy, but said, "And surely I am with you always, to the very end of the age" (Matthew 28:20). Arriving in Canaan Abraham found, to his horror and dismay, famine, disagreeable people, and harsh circumstances. In other words, life was tough. Sometimes it looks and feels as if God is not with us. The journey of the soul to God is not one of happiness or circumstantial bliss, but we are promised his unconditional peace, love, and joy. This can be experienced regardless of the circumstances of our lives. This is the good news.

In Canaan there was a famine in the land, no water for his animals, no food, and life was hard. Discouraged, Abraham lost heart and his dreams were shattered. When this happened I think that he, like us, was thrown back onto the universal memory of early childhood trauma, resonating with his fears of abandonment, rejection, humiliation, or shame. Children are very sensitive to pain but cannot process or grieve pain, so it is repressed and many times does not show itself until we are facing difficulties in our adult lives (chapter 4). Abraham, fearing abandonment, rejection, and humiliation from God, gave in to the dictates of his false self, and was tempted, as a defense, to go to Egypt in search of a better life. Realizing that the Pharaoh would be attracted to his beautiful wife Sarah, and kill him to take her into his harem, he sought protection in his false self. He asked Sarah to act as his sister. We see the deep psycho-spiritual predicament of fallen human beings in that even a man of such great stature and spiritual maturity as Abraham, when faced with the piercing fears of abandonment, rejection and shame, succumbed to the temptation of disobedience, lying and even sacrificing those he loved to protect himself. How many of us, at times, have sold out our family or cheated our children because of our careers or in a mad rush to make that extra dollar?

Promising relief, the false self leads Abraham with his wife to Egypt. Denying our pain and creating for us lives full of illusion, our false selves encourage us to live a lie, or in modern vernacular to recreate reality. Arriving in Egypt, Abraham told the authorities that Sarah was his sister and allowed her to be taken into the Pharaoh's harem. When the Pharaoh found out that Sarah was Abraham's wife and not his sister, he confronted Abraham who shamefully admitted that he had lied. Giving Abraham cattle and returning Sarah, Pharaoh ordered them out of Egypt. The false self promises relief but at the same time causes pain because it is an internal saboteur. Paradoxically we observe this Godly man being chastised by a pagan king about his deceitful behavior and lying attitude.

Humiliated and shamed, Abraham did not let his failure destroy him but instead moved immediately into repentance. Repentance means changing our programs for happiness from those offered by our false selves to find our true security and hope in God (Isaiah 41:10). Returning to Canaan, Abraham re-established his altar, called on God, and pitched his tent. Worshipping God and recognizing that life is transitory, Abraham recommitted himself to the spiritual journey. So often we have the opposite attitude, when we fail we become angry, embittered, or arrogant—but we refuse to repent. As a result we become our own gods and fall prey to the illusions of permanence, sometimes causing still more pain to ourselves and our loved ones. Life is wounded and so we will make mistakes, and we will fall short of principles. We need the courage to admit our wrongdoing, repent by changing our defensive and illusive programs for happiness, and cry out like King David,

> The Lord is my light and my salvation-
> whom shall I fear?
> The Lord is the stronghold of my life-
> of whom shall I be afraid? (Psalm 27:1).

A PEACEMAKER

Shortly after returning to Canaan, conflict arose between the herdsmen of Lot, Abraham's nephew, and Abraham's herdsmen because they felt that the land was not large enough for both of them (Genesis 13:7). I think that Lot, influenced by the wealth and grandeur of Egypt, may have found it difficult to return to the rather harder life in Canaan and to adapt to the uncompromising spirituality of his Uncle Abraham. This would have induced insecurity and ambivalence in his herdsmen, which contributed to the conflict with Abraham's staff. Abraham opened his heart to meet Lot exactly where he was. Abraham had the right to assert his authority and choose whatever land he wanted, but he recognized that God was his sufficiency, and in a loving and compassionate way asked Lot to look to the east and the west, the north and the south and choose the land he wanted. Offering Lot first choice, Abraham took the opposite direction. Influenced by the well-watered plains of Sodom and Gomorrah, which reminded him of the good life of Egypt, Lot chose to pitch his tent just outside those two cities, which had a reputation for wickedness and immorality. Abraham, on the other hand, waited patiently and opened himself to his true self in God, sitting at God's feet. Obviously Abraham had learnt his lesson—it's dangerous to follow the dictates of the false self to defend against the hurt in our hearts and compromise our spirituality. The patriarch had come to a new understanding of the meaning of his life in God and with this insight he gave Lot the first choice. God rewarded Abraham for this, promising him all the land in the surrounding area.

Having made his choice, Abraham relaxed, sitting by the oaks of Mamre. Mamre means fat or pleasantness, and it is a reminder that things have now settled down. It is the kind of calm or peace we experience sometimes in our lives when things are going well. But in the soul's journey to God, we are not allowed to sit beside those still waters for long. I do not profess to know why this is. Maybe we get bored or fall into the illusion that this is our life—that we are the captains of the ship. Or our false selves reassert themselves and we start to be lulled into finding our identities in the *pleasantness*. We so easily forget that, "a man's life is not his own; it is not for man to direct his steps" (Jeremiah 10:23). Then word came to Abraham that his nephew Lot had been captured by some of the kings of Salem who invaded Sodom. From our own experiences we could understand Abraham being very frustrated with Lot, but the contemplative spirit has a great tolerance for understanding and compassion. Although he may have felt angry or discouraged, Abraham made plans to rescue Lot. Gathering about 300 men from his household, Abraham advanced through the night and the rescue was successful.

After the victory, Abraham was met by Melchizedek, the priest of God and King of Salem, who had bread and wine. Recognizing God's servant, Abraham showed his respect for God, bowed to the priest and offered him one tenth of all that he possessed. In victory Abraham was true to his God as the Supreme Being of his life. Appearing before Abraham, the defeated King of Sodom offered Abraham the bounty from his victory. But Abraham refused to take any of this wealth, saying that he did not want it said that the pagan king had made him rich. This is a powerful statement because Abraham by this action stated that his hope, his meaning, was in God and God alone—unlike in former years when he followed his false self into Egypt to seek better conditions. So in a sense, by refusing to take bounty from the King of Salem, Abraham recognized that life is transitory, that all good things come from God alone, the meaning of the tent. We see that in defeat, when he left Egypt, Abraham returned to his altar and tent and now, even in victory, Abraham worshipped God, returning to his altar and his tent. It is important to note, however, that Abraham did not force his conviction to refuse the bounty on his men—he allowed them to exercise their right to be rewarded by the defeated King for risking their lives fighting with him. Contemplative experience respects the rights and convictions of other people; it allows them to make their own decisions. Contemplation leads us to follow our own spiritual journey to God in community with others, but recognizes that we cannot force our convictions on others.

EXPEDIENCY AND GUIDANCE

The word now came to Abraham that he would have a son who would be the rightful heir to his inheritance. The only difficulty was that his wife Sarah was barren. Sarah, choosing expediency, sought to help God by telling Abraham that he could have an affair with their maid, Hagar, and the son resulting from that relationship could become the heir. With the vulnerability of the male sex, Abraham fell prey to Sarah's suggestion and had a child with Hagar. Complying with Sarah, Abraham now had a son, Ishmael, whom he hoped would become the promised heir. This is a very important insight, dare I say lesson, because in contemplation we become aware of the promise of God. If we can't wait or don't have faith to understand, we try to help out God, act out of expediency, and in doing so usurp the authority of God and sometimes create chaos. The life of faith in the spiritual journey is not only accepting the promises of God but also learning to wait, even though we don't see how the promises will be fulfilled. This is easier said than done. We all understand Sarah, who wanted to ensure that the promises of God would be fulfilled. Like us, she was trying to help God. This led to a painful situation that is still with us today, in that the descendents of Ishmael, the Arabs, and the descendents of Isaac, the Jews, still are in major conflict. A powerful conflict developed between Hagar and Sarah with the pregnancy, which resulted in Hagar being sent away. In the wilderness she met an angel who encouraged her to go back to Abraham and Sarah.

So often when things become difficult in our lives, we run away to nowhere. But opening ourselves to God's presence, we often hear him telling us to return to where we belong, go back to the first things, go back to our faith, go back to our simple prayer life, go back to our church, and go back to our fellowship. Often there is pain, but when God calls us to go back, he is not necessarily calling us to the dynamic situation or persons involved. He is calling us to himself. Contemplation means living our lives in God's presence always, as the Apostle Paul says, "He [Jesus] died for us so that, whether we are awake or asleep, we may live together with him" (1 Thessalonians 5:10).

A PROMISE

Years later Abraham was sitting quietly in his tent in the middle of the day when three men appeared. Two of them were angels and the Bible says one was the Lord himself (Genesis 18:1-2). Graciously receiving them, Abraham showered them with hospitality and made them feel very much at home. Contemplation, above all, means opening to the love of God in the world, validated by an open, compassionate and hospitable attitude and in spite of everything, continuing to be kind, giving, and understanding. The visitors told Abraham that in a year's time he and his wife would have a biological heir who would be blessed by God. Meanwhile Sarah, who was standing in the background, was shocked to hear this. Seeing the situation from her own false-self perspective, a rational perspective without faith, Sarah started to laugh. The Lord asked Sarah, "Why are you laughing?" She denied it, saying she was not laughing, but then the Lord asked her a rhetorical question, which was actually a statement: "Is anything too hard for the Lord?"(Genesis 18:14). This question comes to all of us at times in our lives, particularly when we are going through very deep waters and it is hard to see how we can make it. We can be comforted by the question, "Is anything too hard for the Lord?" The Lord says to us, "I have chosen you" (Isaiah 41:9). Sometimes it is very difficult for us to make sense of these words in our modern-day experience with the hustle and bustle and urgent time pressures of our lives. Nevertheless the as Jesus said, "All things are possible with God" (Mark 10:27).

As well as telling Abraham that he would have a son, the angels also said that God could no longer tolerate the wickedness of Sodom and Gomorrah and would destroyed them. After all the ups and downs with Lot, we would not be surprised if Abraham had said to himself, "I've done my part. I rescued Lot from the King of Salem, I did my best for him, but in spite of everything he returned to live in Sodom and Gomorrah." But the very heart of the meaning of contemplation is compassion. Abraham may still have been very fed up with Lot, but he was also compassionate. And so Abraham bargained with God. It is a touching sight where God the Infinite One relates to and bargains with a finite human person. Abraham bargained with God to save the city if there were fifty righteous people, and then he continued the bargaining process down to ten. I wonder why Abraham didn't bargain further, but being a very spiritual person who feared God, maybe Abraham realized that if God was willing to move from fifty down to ten, this was more than reasonable. The tragedy is that there weren't even ten godly people and so Sodom and Gomorrah were destroyed.

When we look at the wickedness or evil of a civilization or even a country, it is important to bear in mind that God made it very clear that this destruction of Sodom and Gomorrah took place not just because of the evil but because there was an insufficient remnant of people who were seeking to serve him. This means that the faith of the remnant is extremely important. Our faith not only blesses our family, it blesses our neighborhood, it blesses our country, and it affects the world. The remnant of faith is a healing balm in the midst of our modern culture. My point is that when God looks at the world he does not just look at evil or negativity, he looks at those people who are trying to follow him. Though there is evil in the world, and much wrongdoing, there is still hope because if we choose to follow our Lord, many will benefit. Let us not then be discouraged. Wives do not give up on your husbands. Husbands do not give up on your wives. Parents keep on trying with your children. Let us keep struggling with the difficult social problems of our culture.

Before destroying the city, the angels went to Sodom and Gomorrah, and there they visited Lot who invited them back to his home (Genesis 19:1-3). Demonstrating kindness and hospitality Lot, like his uncle Abraham, made his guests feel very much at home. But because of the violence in the city, young and old men accosted Lot's household to attack his visitors. Lot, distressed by the whole process, offered them his two virgin daughters in exchange. There is something very, very painful here. Things had become so debauched that Lot was willing to give up his two virgin daughters to satisfy the lust of the masses. But God is still on the throne, so the men that were visiting, recognizing the hopelessness of the situation, blinded the mob and pulled Lot inside. They told Lot to prepare to leave by morning, because Sodom and Gomorrah would be destroyed.

Despite all that had happened, Lot was resistant and had to be pulled out of Sodom and Gomorrah with his wife and two daughters, while his sons-in-law stayed. The angels told them not to look back, but Lot's wife, like so many of us, was unable to say goodbye to what she was used to: friends, social clubs, wealth or what have you. She looked back and fell into a tar pit, turning to a pillar of salt. Eventually Lot ended up in a cave with his two daughters and in a very sad, painful story they got him drunk, had sex with him, and later gave birth to two children who became the ancestors of the Amorites and the Moabites, two cultures that the Bible says became like Sodom and Gomorrah. This tragic story illustrates how we may take the girls out of Sodom but it is hard to take Sodom out of the girls. It reminds us as families, as parents, as concerned citizens, how important it is to create a healing and constructive environment for children.

TESTING

In a very deep sense, contemplation means a willingness to be tested by God. God called Abraham to face a test of the authenticity of his altar, that is his ultimate concern. God is always testing our altar, because the altar is the place where our true selves abide in God. Without the altar, we succumb to our false selves, which are associated with illusive programs for happiness, idols, and addictions. The altar must be kept intact because without it we forget that we live in a tent, and we create an illusion of permanence. So in this story God asked Abraham to sacrifice his beloved heir Isaac. This is mystery and we can only imagine the pain and conflict experienced by Abraham. But, being faithful, Abraham obeyed God and took his son, his only son Isaac, to Mount Moriah to sacrifice him, perhaps in some way hoping that God would redeem even the most tragic circumstances (Genesis 22:2). The journey to Mount Moriah is always a painful process in our lives. But sadly, no one can go to a deeper experience of contemplation without walking their own journey to Mount Moriah. Sometimes it involves a particular illness, the failure of a business, depression, or some kind of problem with our children or family, but all of us, some way or the other, as we open ourselves to the deeper aspect of our spiritual journey, will find our way to Mount Moriah. Even our Lord Jesus Christ in the Garden of Gethsemane cried, "My Father, if it is possible, may this cup be taken from me. Yet not as I will, but as you will" (Matthew 26:39).

At a certain point Abraham came to the place on the journey to Mount Moriah where he told those accompanying them to stay put while he and his son went forth to worship. Abraham called the testing of God worship (Genesis 22:5). This is always a sign of deep spiritual maturity. Worship is the only grace we have in life, it is the only thing we can really do, it is the duty of all human beings because in this life we can never be satisfied fully, neither can we obtain God fully, but in the midst of these two forces we are called upon to worship God and to glorify him forever. As we worship God, we acknowledge that we are made in his image. We recognize that he is in charge of our lives. As David says, "My soul finds rest in God alone; my salvation comes from him" (Psalm 62:1).

The experience of testing is always to clarify and purify the presence of God in our lives and open our hearts to worship. Worship is the screening process God places on our lives to separate out the dross of the false self—attachments and addictions—leaving God alone with our true selves in him. At the time of testing it is important to call upon God, who is the God of all comfort, and to realize that he is calling us to himself in worship, to experience being alone with the Alone, the one and only true God. Sometimes testing discourages us; it may or may not be followed by growth. God tests us in order to bless us and to reveal the mystery of his love to us. Faithful to God's test, Abraham is promised a special blessing for himself, his family, his descendants, in fact the whole world. If we are willing to walk faithfully with God in the testing, it purifies our hearts and opens us to deeper blessings.

Contemplation always involves purification, and purification means our hearts come under the scrutiny of God's piercing eyes so that our selfishness is removed and we accept our total dependence on him "Blessed are the pure in heart, for they will see God" (Matthew 5:8). But most importantly, God was revealing a blue print of his eternal plan for the redemption of the world in the giving of his only son, the Lord Jesus Christ, to be the sacrificial lamb for the sins and pain of the world. Taking Abraham into his confidence, God was revealing to him the salvation of the world. As Abraham is about to sacrifice Isaac the angel stops his hand and provides the lamb. God was showing Abraham that he would give his son Jesus Christ, but at that point there would be no hand to stop the onslaught of the cruel crown of thorns, the piercing spear, the beating, and the shame. Jesus the savior of the world died for our sins, but he also rose triumphant from the grave, bringing hope and salvation to the world.

Testing is never easy but it must be seen in the context of God the lover revealing himself to us, the beloved. In essence God is love and as we continue our journey toward contemplation we, like Abraham, will journey to our own Mount Moriah. Some reading this book may be going through such experience now. May God give us grace to experience his presence and love. Testing is hard, it is tough, it is lonely, but God is with us. Earlier on in Abraham's life, when he felt discouraged and maybe afraid after conquering the kings of Salem, God spoke to him so beautifully saying, "Do not be afraid, Abram. I am your shield, your very great reward" (Genesis 15:1). How important it is for us to realize that God calls us to himself as an antidote to fear. Reminding us that he is the one who really protects us, he also warns us and encourages us to recognize that he himself, and he alone, is our reward. In other words, we seek God who gives us consolation, rather than seeking consolation and finding God. God himself is the desire of our hearts. We all long to see the face of God, for it is in his image that we are made. We belong to God (Psalm 17:15).

SARAH'S DEATH

Abraham had a deep, loving relationship with his beautiful wife Sarah. Sarah started off her life being called Sari, which means contentious. But as she continued her journey to God, he changed her name to Sarah, meaning princess. Life is about growing our souls and Sarah's growth through the grace of her spiritual journey is an excellent example, challenging us to move from a contentious to a serene spirit. Pausing briefly, let us ask what development is taking place in our lives as we continue our spiritual journey. Sarah is celebrated as a person of faith because of her trust and willingness to follow God. This does not mean that she was faultless, but I think that the common theme of her life was not a focus on her failures but a commitment to be open to God's love and guidance.

It is very touching how Abraham grieved—he came to mourn for Sarah and to weep for her (Genesis 23:2). In those days the corpse was put in a special tent and the bereaved husband would kneel down before the corpse. Grieving for Sarah, Abraham knelt down and gave thanks and appreciation for the faithfulness and commitment of his dear wife. Most touching of all is the fact that even though Abraham was offered Sarah's tomb free of charge, he refused to accept it. He wanted to buy the tomb as a statement of faith that his descendents would inherit the land. During his lifetime, the only land that Abraham owned was the land he bought for Sarah's tomb. As Abraham counted out the pieces of silver and bought the tomb, he powerfully demonstrated his love and commitment. So often in our lives we do not see the fulfillment of God's promises, but the challenge is to live in faith and hope, with the will to serve God and bow to his will, trusting in the fulfillment of his promises for us in his own time and space.

A COSMIC DANCE OF LOVE

According to the Judeo-Christian perspective, we are made in the image of God. God is love, which involves the good (doing), the true (knowing), and the beautiful (feeling). Our true essence is to live and love. We come from love, to love, to be in love, and return to love. Life then is the cosmic dance of love with God the lover, the hound of heaven, seeking us the beloved. But life is wounded. God the lover reached out to us through his son, Jesus Christ, to liberate us from the futility and the destruction of our false selves. Jesus reminds us that if we are to follow him we must deny ourselves (our false selves), take up our crosses (face the reality of our pain and failure before God) and follow him (accept his sacrifice and forgiveness); then we will find our true selves in God. This is a continual challenge for all of us.

Near the end of Abraham's life we see that he sought to live in love as opposed to addiction. He had a deep love for others: his father Terah, Sarah his wife, Isaac, Hagar and Ishmael and of course Lot. He depended on God for his security; he refused to take money from the pagan king of Salem, but instead gave one tenth of what he had to God. Abraham was patient. After receiving the promise from God that his descendants would bless the earth, he had to learn to wait for the fulfillment. Abraham listened intently, which allowed him an increased awareness of God who told him, "Do not be afraid, I am your shield, your very great reward" (Genesis 15:1). He was compassionate even though Lot had chosen Sodom and Gomorrah, and risked his life to rescue him. Sadly, Lot returned to Sodom. Then when Abraham heard that Sodom and Gomorrah were going to be destroyed, he bargained with God hoping to save Lot and his family. He was able to grieve. This is always a sign of love because we can only grieve as deeply as we love, and we can only love as deeply as we grieve. He grieved deeply for Sarah at her death and demonstrated faith and respect by purchasing a special burial ground for her and his ancestors. He was committed to his son Isaac, his biological heir, and he had a special love for Ishmael, the son of Hagar.

Living life to the fullest, Abraham was satisfied. His life was filled with adventure, challenge, blessing, and faith. Known as a friend of God, Abraham lived by faith in spite of the circumstances (Hebrews 11:8). Abraham reminds us that the experience of contemplation gives us an awareness of God in our lives and in the world. Contemplation also leads us beyond this life into the eternal presence of God in death. When Abraham died it was said that he was gathered to his people (Genesis 25:8). Many years later when the Sadducees, a religious sect who did not believe in the resurrection of the dead, asked Jesus a question about life after death, Jesus said, "God said ... 'I am the God of Abraham, the God of Isaac, and the God of Jacob.' He is not the God of the dead, but of the living. You are badly mistaken!" (Mark 12:26-27). In the story of the poor beggar Lazarus and the rich man, Jesus said that after death Lazarus rested at the side of Abraham, a place of fellowship in the presence of God (Luke 16:22). Abraham's life speaks to us not only of life on planet earth but also reveals much about the afterlife. We are reminded that life does not end with death. There is a great crowd of witnesses in the eternal realm where contemplation, or being with God, continues forever.

CONCLUSION

Abraham can be understood as demonstrating the power of contemplation in the soul's journey to God. Abraham's willingness to empty himself and be filled with the spirit led to a transformation of consciousness that enabled him to live from an interior space, with God's spirit living and praying in him. Thus he was a blessing to his family, his descendants and the whole world. Patriarch of three major world religions, Abraham is a powerful guide for our own spiritual journeys. He reminds us that we have to let go of the old ways. He reminds us that we have to face tests and trials—these are not easy. He reminds us that we sometimes fail no matter how hard we try. But most of all he reminds us that when we fail, we can repent and try again and again rather than become angry and lose hope! Abraham reminds us that this life points to another life beyond. Life is a symbol, a bridge crossing to an unseen shore—the kingdom of love.

As we travel along life's sorrowing main we can take hope from Abraham and try, try, and try again. Abraham's life illustrates both the spiritual maturity of seeking God, but also the reality of human failure. But each time, he bowed before God and repented. He had a deep love for his son Ishmael, and when Sarah was angry with Ishmael and his mother Hagar, Abraham was compassionate and wanted to make peace.

At Abraham's funeral both sons, Isaac and Ishmael, came together to bury him (Genesis 25:9). What a beautiful image—Isaac representing the Jewish people and Ishmael representing the Arab people came together to show respect for their beloved father, reminding us of our common heritage. This is our dream and hope that as Isaac and Ishmael came together in recognition of their common fatherhood, so we can reunite and rediscover peace in the Middle East. Abraham's life reminds us that we cannot only dream of this, but must step out to follow the voice of love through ups and downs, resistance, and discouragement.

According to Feiler,

> The true meaning of Abraham's death cannot be
> diminished. Abraham achieves in death what he could
> never achieve in life: a moment of reconciliation between
> his two sons, a peaceful, communal, side-by-side flicker
> of possibility in which they are not rivals, scions,
> warriors, adversaries, children, Jews, Christians, or
> Muslims. They are brothers. They are mourners.[4]

In a sense these two sons are us, forever weeping for the loss of our common father, shuffling through our bitter memories, reclaiming our childlike expectations, smiling, laughing, sobbing, furious and full of dreams, wondering about our orphaned future, and demanding the answers we all crave to hear: What did you want from me Father? What did you leave me with, Father?

> But this Abraham believes against all belief – that his
> children still crave God. They still need the comfort of
> something greater than themselves, still hold on to some
> gleam of humanity, still dream of a moment when they
> stand alongside one another and pray for their lost father
> and for the legacy of peace among the nations that was
> his initial mandate from Heaven.[5]

Abraham's life is a beautiful statement of the soul's journey to God in the midst of life. May we, as we look at his life, see the little lights that could help to light up the darkness of our lives and give us courage to travel our personal spiritual journeys. Through it all, God is with us and speaks as he did to Abraham saying, "Do not be afraid" (Genesis 15:1). This is a command. Knowing God is the antidote to fear. He says, "I am your shield" (Genesis 15:1). God's protection is around us, he is with us, and nothing can touch us unless he allows it. And finally God says, "I am your very great reward" (Genesis 15:1). So often we look for the consolations of God and the benefits of seeking God or knowing God, but God warns us that what our human hearts really desire is not what God can give us, but God himself. It is only as we move deeper into contemplation that we recognize that in the awareness of his presence and love all our issues, questions, and doubts pale to insignificance; God himself, God alone is our consolation, our hope and our reward! As Abraham taught and showed, our divine duty is to live, glorify, serve and enjoy God forever and ever.

REFERENCES

1. Father John quoted by Bruce Feiler in *Abraham: A Journey to the Heart of Three Faiths* (New York: William Morrow HarperCollins Publishers Inc., 2002), 50.

2. Ray C. Stedman, *Man of Faith* (Portland: Multnomah Press, 1971), 41-42.

3. Bruce Feiler, *Abraham: A Journey to the Heart of Three Faiths* (New York: William Morrow HarperCollins Publishers Inc., 2002), 218.

4. Bruce Feiler, *Abraham: A Journey to the Heart of Three Faiths* (New York: William Morrow HarperCollins Publishers Inc., 2002), 208.

5. Bruce Feiler, *Abraham: A Journey to the Heart of Three Faiths* (New York: William Morrow HarperCollins Publishers Inc., 2002), 217-18.

CHAPTER 8
DAVID: CONTEMPLATION AND REJECTION

How lovely is your dwelling place, O Lord Almighty! My soul yearns, even faints, for the courts of the Lord; my heart and my flesh cry out for the living God. (Psalm 84:1-2)

The weary King David paused to look back as he trudged sorrowfully up the Mount of Olives, weeping with each step. Behind him, across the Kidron valley, lay the city of Jerusalem, with its magnificent temple and palace, from which he had suddenly been forced to flee. After years of great success at home and on the battlefield, David was facing the supreme challenge of his career. None of the enemies of Israel had ever succeeded in mounting a serious threat to his kingdom, but now it was being overturned and his life was in mortal danger—not from an external threat but from his own beloved son Absalom!

Like David, most of us have tasted the bitterness of defeat in some area of our lives. Defeat may take the form of a failed relationship, serious illness, disappointment in business affairs, or continual defeat in the grip of some secret compulsion. In this chapter I suggest a ten-step process through which we, like David, can seek the inner healing that will enable us to move to ever-deeper levels of intimacy.

So often contemplation has a soft ring to it, conjuring up visions of spineless persons focusing on pie in the sky and denying the blood and guts of every day living. Yet David is described as Israel's greatest king, a consummate warrior, leader, musician, and poet (1 and 2 Samuel). Contemplation opens us to the vision of God's love, and is validated by a courageous, compassionate, and uncompromising commitment to intimacy in the world. David was far from perfect; he made wrong decisions and suffered the consequences of his actions, yet through his mistakes, David sought deep contemplation and intimacy with God. He is the only one who God called "a man after my own heart" (Acts 13:22). Absalom was the pride of David's life, a young man who, like his father, was attractive and highly gifted: "In all Israel there was not a man so highly praised for his handsome appearance as Absalom. From the top of his head to the sole of his foot there was no blemish in him" (2 Samuel 14:25).

Absalom, however, lacked David's character. In time his arrogant and ruthless side surfaced and he coveted the throne of his own father. He schemed to win the affection of the people by assuming the trappings of royalty, riding through the streets of Jerusalem in a majestic chariot with fifty men running before him. He would sit in a prominent place at the city gate and hear grievances, exclaiming: "If only I were appointed judge in the land! Then everyone who has a complaint or case could come to me and I would see that he gets justice" (2 Samuel 15:4). Like any good politician Absalom employed an intensive PR campaign to promote his cause. Some politicians kiss babies, but Absalom, in a slavish demonstration of mock deference, kissed the hands of those who came to him. Flattered by the aspiring king who deferred to them, the populace flocked to Absalom, and we read that, "He stole the hearts of the men of Israel" (2 Samuel 15:6). When Absalom felt he had garnered sufficient popular support he made his move. Its amazing how gullible parents can be. It seems that David did not suspect that his son was planning to usurp his very throne. And so when Absalom asked to be allowed to go to the city of Hebron for a spiritual retreat, David readily agreed, perhaps thinking, "At last Absalom is showing an interest in spiritual things!" What a brutal shock it must have been to be told that Absalom was leading a rebellion against him and that all Israel seemed eager to follow. Hebron was but a day's hard march away, and David realized he had no choice but to flee for his life.

1. RECOGNIZE THE PROBLEM

Each of us needs to do what David did when his world collapsed: face up to the reality of life. He was no longer king and there was no use pretending he was still ruler over Israel. Absalom had overthrown him. The naiveté with which David had glossed over his son's faults dissipated suddenly as he warned his loyal followers: "Come! We must flee, or none of us will escape from Absalom. We must leave immediately, or he will move quickly to overtake us and bring ruin upon us and put the city to the sword" (2 Samuel 15:14).

We are all tempted to fall back on certain typical defense mechanisms which prevent us from facing up to the truth. One of these is denial, as in: "Oh my little boy Absalom would never do anything like this!" It's a good thing David didn't delude himself because the results could have been fatal. Denial means that hurts are never dealt with and can be passed along from generation to generation. We find ourselves hurting our children in ways we ourselves were damaged by our parents. The first step to breaking the power of denial is by facing up to the deep hurt in our hearts.

Another natural defensive reaction is projection, allowing ourselves to be caught up in the endless if only introspective cycle of wishful thinking: If only Absalom were more loyal; If only I hadn't married her I would never be in this mess; If only I had never met him, this wouldn't have happened; If only I'd never taken this job. Projection puts the blame squarely on someone else's shoulders. We blame others, circumstances, an organization, the government, or even inanimate objects, anything but ourselves.

I remember how once, after having a couple of wisdom teeth removed, complications set in. Unable to go to my dentist, I tried an over-the-counter medication to ease the considerable discomfort. I found that this topical medication indeed relieved the pain as advertised—but it did so only for a brief period of time. I had to apply it continually to keep the pain at bay. Projection is like this. It makes us feel better to be able to blame someone or something else for our problems—but it only works for a while, it can never produce healing. Healing only comes when we take our part of the responsibility for the wounds in our hearts. We may be the cause of only a very small part of the hurt we have suffered. We may have no responsibility at all for wounds that were caused in us as children, but as adults we do have a responsibility to work through the resulting hurt and pain. Healing begins when we own our portion of the responsibility.

2. FACE REALITY

When David was devastated by the news of Absalom's revolt, he faced up to the reality of his situation and took action, even if it meant the embarrassment of open flight from his own son. Perhaps, as he fled across the Mount of Olives, David pondered the defeats of some of his illustrious forefathers. It is enlightening to see how many of the great men of faith in the Bible experienced significant failure in their lifetimes. Moses, for example, fled Egypt at the age of forty in fear of his life after killing an Egyptian. He spent the next forty years as a humble shepherd in the desert, at the end of which he was probably thinking his career was just about over. But it was just beginning. At the age of eighty God called Moses to lead the children of Israel on their epic journey out of Egypt to the Promised Land.

Putting things in perspective means facing up to the reality of our situation, however unpleasant it may be. For David it meant flight into the desert, the last thing he would have envisioned. But his very life was at stake. We also have to gain the proper perspective when facing serious problems. It means being willing to abandon the ineffectual half-hearted remedies that we have been desperately hoping might be sufficient to bring the needed change. Our situation may require that we, like David, take drastic action such as a change of employment or geographic separation from a dysfunctional family, an abusive spouse, or fellow drug abusers.

3. DON'T GO IT ALONE

At critical times of his life, David surrounded himself with faithful friends who helped and supported him. As a young man fleeing for his life from Saul, he gathered a band of loyal men around him in the wilderness. And here again, many years later, David does not find himself alone. One of these faithful friends is Ittai the Gittite, who accompanies him on his flight from Absalom. When David tries to dissuade him, Ittai replies, "As surely as the Lord lives, and as my lord the king lives, wherever my lord the king

may be, whether it means life or death, there will your servant be"
(2 Samuel 15:21).

Often, it is not pain itself that we find so unbearable, but rather the
lack of love and support we experience during our suffering. Friendship
and community are vital for helping us through our difficulties. No man is
an island; each of us—without exception—needs friendship. We may have
been hurt and lonely for so long that we even try to tell ourselves we
don't need anyone else, but deep inside we long for a friend. The practice
of contemplative prayer calls us to solitude, solitude in companionship
with God. But true solitude always leads to meaningful communion and
community. As we consent to the presence and action of God's love in our
life, he places significant persons around us to support, guide and represent his loving care.

How do we find a friend or a support group—a *community*—to stand
with us? In my experience we find friends when we are willing to come
out of hiding and seek healthy relationships. It is a hard first step to take.
The fear of rejection is a powerful inhibitor that can keep people in their
shells for much of their lifetimes. Others are not attracted to us when we
are withdrawn. We give the impression of being unfriendly, of not being
interested in others, and suffer further rejection as others in turn avoid us.
Taking the risk of opening ourselves up breaks the vicious cycle that only
leads to deeper loneliness. It begins the process of unleashing the healing
forces within our hearts. I can hear the protest: "But I lack the natural
charisma or attractiveness of a David. How can I find friends?" Finding a
good friend is one of the most essential yet most difficult tasks in our
modern, isolated society. The book of Proverbs gives us a simple yet effective rule for finding friends: "A man of many companions may come to
ruin, but there is a friend who sticks closer than a brother"
(Proverbs 18:24).

Some people have great difficulty finding friends because they are not
friendly. They do not show genuine interest in others but appear to be only
interested in finding a "pin cushion" on whom to unload their troubles. But
friendship is a two-way street. If we take the time to listen genuinely to
others, then we will find other people with a willingness to give us the
support that we need. One of the most rewarding ways to find friendship
is belonging to a social group—the key is finding a healthy and supportive
community. Many of us got into trouble in the first place by, as the song

goes, "looking for love in all the wrong places". We were desperately seeking friendship, but only in the social groups where we thought we could find acceptance. Instead of true friendship we found ourselves entrapped in harmful or illicit behavior.

Perhaps the best way to begin to find supportive community is to rediscover your own family. Spend time together; begin to rebuild broken relationships and nurture one another. Work on renewing your relationships with your relatives, especially if you are single. Another excellent place to find supportive community is in a friendly and open church. Religious communities are ideally suited to meet both our spiritual and our social needs, although religious communities that were not friendly have hurt some people. Other good sources of potential friends are groups organized around contemplative prayer.b Theses provide a focus and unleash God's unfailing love. You will probably experience a few false starts on your road to finding a friend, but don't give up! If we remember the twin rules of being friendly to others and avoiding unhealthy social communities we will, in time, discover genuine friendship. Unhealthy communities are characterized by non-mutual relationships and by being seductively easy to enter, but complex or difficult to leave.

4. LOOK UPWARDS

As David fled over the Mount of Olives he recognized the hand of God upon his life. Zadok and his fellow priests started to follow carrying the Ark of the Covenant, but were turned back by David who told them: "Take the ark of God back into the city. If I find favor in the Lord's eyes, he will bring me back and let me see it and his dwelling place again" (2 Samuel 15:25). However, he hastened to add that if God should reject him, "then I am ready; let him do to me whatever seems good to him" (2 Samuel 15:26). In the contemplative experience we live in God, for God, and under God's influence.

The wonderful thing about being in relationship with God is that we don't have to play God ourselves. We recognize the existence of one who is greater than us and is ultimately in control, and no longer have to pretend to be in control of everything. Contemplation means opening ourselves to the vision of God's love and committing ourselves to the mission of his love in the world. Life is not hopeless because there is someone who cares: we can become vulnerable and move into intimacy in the confidence that he is watching over us and guiding us.

David was broken, he didn't know how it would all end—but he trusted in God. When our world is shattered, we need someone to help us out of our despair, to give us hope. The God of the Bible represents what many of us have lacked in our earthly families: stability and consistency. In Psalm 23 God is pictured as a kind, caring shepherd who lovingly watches over his sheep: "The Lord is my shepherd, I shall not be in want. He makes me lie down in green pastures, he leads me beside quiet waters" (Psalm 23:1-2). As times of trouble once again threatened to overwhelm him, David threw himself unreservedly into the care of his shepherd. God is consistent in his loving, merciful, just nature, but we can never predict how he will act. Our ways are not his ways (Isaiah 55:8), but still we can trust him as Job did when he said, "Though he slay me, yet will I hope in him" (Job 13:15). This doesn't mean that Job expected God to act cruelly towards him. Far from it: Job is saying that whatever happens, he can rely on his Maker. It is hearing afresh God's word to the patriarch Abraham, "Do not be afraid, I am your shield, your very great reward" (Genesis 15:1).

5. EXPRESS YOURSELF

David seemed to have the ability to express his feelings openly, a trait which helped earn him the love of his people. But David's wife, Michal, felt uncomfortable with any expression of emotion. Years earlier she became greatly offended when she saw him celebrate the arrival of the Ark of the Covenant: "As the ark of the LORD was entering the City of David, Michal daughter of Saul watched from a window. And when she saw King David leaping and dancing before the Lord, she despised him in her heart" (2 Samuel 6:16). As David fled from Absalom, once again he did not hide his emotions: "But David continued up the Mount of Olives, weeping as he went; his head was covered and he was barefoot" (2 Samuel 15:30). Contemplation means being real. If we are hurt we don't have to pretend, but are free to express our feelings to God, regardless of how painful they are.

Our culture may have taught us to expect our leaders to control their emotions and maintain a "stiff upper lip" in the face of adversity. Instead of weeping with others, we may try to change the subject to something more comfortable or, failing that, offer empty platitudes like "Don't worry about it," or "Just hang in there." A gentleman told me that when his wife died during a church service, his fellow church members sought to comfort him with pious admonitions and a litany of Bible verses. But the only balm for his intense grief came later when he arrived back home, and his Haitian gardener came to him crying, showing by his tears how sorry he was to hear about the woman's death. Many of us have difficulty facing our feelings, and so we forfeit experiencing the healing cleansing of tears that flow when the emotional dams in our hearts are released. Not so David! He made no effort to conceal the pain he was feeling as he covered his head and wept bitterly. He set the example for those with him, for we read: "All the people with him covered their heads too and were weeping as they went up" (2 Samuel 15:30).

David was able to face his feelings, and by so doing he was demonstrating his great love for his son Absalom. Grief and love may seem to be opposite feelings but in truth they are connected (chapter 2). Grief is called the healing feeling because the depth of our grief indicates the depth of our ability to love. We cannot have one without the other, and so we must allow ourselves to feel the pain when our world is broken and those we love hurt us.

6. REPENT

This is not a common word in the modern vernacular. In essence it means changing our attitudes and opening our hearts to God. The word for repentance, *metanoia,* literally means to turn. David's attitude, as he walked up the mountain with bare feet and a covered head, was one of open repentance. In his pain, he opened his life to God (2 Samuel 15:30).

King David's dream of power and respect as a king with a cohesive and loving family was shattered when his son Absalom usurped the throne and threatened his life. Abandoned, rejected and humiliated, King David faced his past failings, accepted defeat, and humbled himself before God in repentance. Trusting only in the mercy of God, he turned away from his false-self defenses of denial and projection, which create the illusion of security, power, and invincibility. He was vulnerable, left only with his true identity as a person beloved by God. Our previous discussions of the false and true selves (chapters 4 and 6) are poignantly illustrated by this painful period in David's life.

Jesus had an amazing saying that runs contrary to our aggressive, power-oriented culture: "Anyone who will not receive the kingdom of God like a little child will never enter it" (Luke 18:17). That's repentance—to open up our inner child to God. It means becoming vulnerable as a child, asking him to touch us so that we can respond to his love as a little child would. Like a trusting child we need an inner flexibility so that we can bend as we go through the inner turning of repentance. A true adult is someone who bends rather than breaks when they come to a point of change in their lives.

Often with us there is another dynamic that prevents us from opening up to God in our time of deepest need—that of transference: attributing qualities from a significant person in our lives to others, in this case God. For better or worse, our human parents and other authority figures become our models for understanding God. If those human relationships are marred and we are angry about them, these feelings are displaced onto God and can profoundly affect how we relate to our Heavenly Father. Instead of seeing God as kind and loving, we may envision him as cold, distant, or someone to be feared. And so our woundedness causes us to turn away from God rather than to accept his unconditional love.

Life is meant to be an adventure and we should cultivate a childlike enthusiasm for learning. As painful as tragedies are, they can be the optimum time for growth. Suffering forces us to face ourselves—both our strengths and our weaknesses—and to confront the issues in our lives. Repentance can turn a crisis into an opportunity for profound transformation.

7. SEEK HELP

When David came to the top of the mountain his friend, General Hushai, came to meet him in mourning "his robe torn and dust on his head" (2 Samuel 15:32). This may seem odd to us, but Hushai was demonstrating his shock and sorrow over David's misfortune. He was in effect saying, "Master, I love you. What can I do to help?" He was loyal, committed, and willing to help.

David was in desperate need of assistance. He devised a plan whereby Hushai returned to Jerusalem and frustrated Absalom's plans to pursue and capture David. David wasn't afraid to ask for help when he needed it and neither should we be. Contemplation is not living in denial, but facing the real in all that is real. This means being willing to reach out and seek professional help when needed. When we are looking for someone to help, we need a Hushai. Look for someone who is able to show genuine love and concern who, like Hushai, comes with a heart of humility and gentleness. The test of true contemplation is genuine friendship—a commitment to the love that is stronger than death.

8. BEWARE OF SHIMEI

As David continued on his journey he was accosted by a rascal named Shimei, who cursed him and shouted: "Get out, get out, you man of blood, you scoundrel! The Lord has repaid you for all the blood you shed in the household of Saul, in whose place you have reigned. The Lord has handed the kingdom over to your son Absalom. You have come to ruin because you are a man of blood!" (2 Samuel 16:7-8).

Like David, we all suffer from the internal Shimei syndrome, which kicks us when we are down, condemning us in the midst of our defeats. When we seek intimacy, to confront the issues in our hearts, the accusing voices chime in: "What are you doing this for? You can't do that! You'll never amount to anything." Along comes projection: "If you'd been a better parent he wouldn't have turned out like this..., If you weren't such a poor excuse for a wife, he wouldn't have left you..." The Shimeis of our lives can be external as well. Those who have suffered misfortune know all too well how so-called friends can gossip behind our backs and remind us to our face of our failures. Few injuries are more painful than being hurt by someone when we are already as low as we can get. Once burned, twice shy. It is no wonder why so many—even in our churches—no longer reach out, for fear of encountering another "Job's comforter".

One of David's soldiers, Abishai, decided enough was enough and asked permission to lop off the scoundrel Shimei's head. But David would have none of it, and told Abishai, "My son, who is of my own flesh, is trying to take my life. How much more, then, this Benjamite! Leave him alone; let him curse, for the Lord has told him to. It may be that the Lord will see my

distress and repay me with good for the cursing I am receiving today"
(2 Samuel 16:11-12). This sense of forbearing and understanding at a time
when we are being maligned is one of the hallmarks of the
contemplative spirit.

Here we see the spiritual depth of David and his complete dependence upon God. He had lost everything, and a worthless nobody was openly humiliating him. But David refused to exact revenge upon Shimei. He
knew that he might well deserve some of the punishment he was experiencing. David, being a true contemplative, instead of either excusing or
accusing himself wisely trusted his future wholly to God—the love that
will never let us go, and the face that never turns away.

Meanwhile back in Jerusalem, General Hushai arrived at the court of
Absalom just as Ahithophel, another of David's former counselors, was
advising the new king on how to deal with David. Ahithophel recommend-
ed that he himself be given a strong contingent of soldiers with which to
pursue David immediately. It was sound counsel and Absalom was inclined
to accept it but decided to ask Hushai's advice. Hushai subverted the
advice of Ahithophel by appealing to Absalom's innate narcissism. Should
another lead the attack against David? "No!" counseled Hushai, suggesting
that Absalom should wait until tomorrow and then have the honor of
defeating his father himself, thus establishing his right to his throne!
Absalom accepted Hushai's advice and the extra time allowed David and
his men to escape (2 Samuel 17:5-14). As a footnote to this incident,
Ahithophel showed his rigidity in dealing with rejection by tragically going
out and hanging himself (2 Samuel 17:23).

Ahithophel's co-dependence with the PIP – or party in power proved
fatal. When David ruled, Ahithophel sided with him, but when the PIP
changed he quickly changed his allegiance. But when the new PIP rejected
him, there was nowhere left to turn which caused him to despair. It is the
same with us when we entrust others with our "MDIV" – Meaning, Dignity,
Identity, and Value – card and look to them to give us meaning and value.
Disillusionment will inevitably set in as others fail us.

9. TAKE APPROPRIATE ACTION

That evening Hushai sent word secretly to David of Absalom's plans to pursue him the next day. David moved immediately and he and his men

escaped that very night. He then planned his attack, dividing his army into three groups for battle. Contemplation is not passive acquiescence, but moving with God's guidance into action.

After we have isolated the problem and faced our hurts, grieved and done the work of repenting, there comes a time for action. Sometimes, instead of making plans and setting goals for self-improvement, we hold back, fearful of taking that first step. Just as it is impossible to steer a car that isn't moving, we cannot realize the change we desire unless we are taking concrete steps. Even if we suffer some initial setbacks, we cannot help but succeed in the end—if we persevere. What steps are we taking right now to help bring change into our lives?

My wife Vicki is painfully aware of my own shortcomings in this area. She has a friend married to a Dutchman who can fix anything. If the washing machine breaks down, she just calls her husband and he's there in a minute to fix it. But when our washing machine breaks down and Vicki calls me, my response is: "Well, how do you feel about it?" We can talk ceaselessly about what has gone wrong and how we feel about it, but sooner or later we have to take action and fix the washing machine.

Another pitfall is setting goals that are unworkable. At first David unrealistically insisted on leading his men into battle against Absalom, but he was older and his fighting days were over. Besides, David's men doubted that he had the resolve to do battle against his own son and they prevail upon him to stay back. David accepted the pleas of his generals that he not endanger himself by accompanying them into battle. He was willing to listen to good advice. In the same way, we need to listen to good advice and be practical in our objectives. Many goals are not attained because they bear so little resemblance to reality that we never seriously attempt to accomplish them. It is better to set a modest, workable goal rather than a grandiose scheme that doesn't have a prayer of being realized.

Absalom soon found himself in a situation for which he had no strategy. After the battle began he was riding on his donkey through the thick of the forest when the long hair for which he was famous became ensnared in the branches of an oak tree. His mule continued on, leaving Absalom hanging between heaven and earth. When tragedy hits and the bottom drops out of our lives, we experience the same feeling of helplessness. Absalom apparently had not prepared himself for such an eventuality and was paralyzed when the unexpected occurred. This was his downfall.

10. BE COMPASSIONATE

Absalom was spotted by one of David's soldiers, who told his commander, Joab. Now Joab had a long and turbulent history, and would eventually himself fall by the sword (1 Kings 2:34). He was angry when he learned that the soldier had not killed Absalom when he had the chance. The soldier had spunk, and stood up to Joab, replying, "Even if a thousand shekels were weighed out into my hands, I would not lift my hand against the king's son. In our hearing the king commanded you and Abishai and Ittai, 'Protect the young man Absalom for my sake.'" (2 Samuel 18:12). Joab brushed aside what the soldier said; grabbed three spears, and rushed off to kill Absalom. David, ignorant of what had happened, waited eagerly for news of the battle and especially of the fate of his son. When the messenger arrived he had only one question: "Is the young man Absalom safe?" (2 Samuel 18:32). David was a powerful warrior and a great king, but he was also a father. Despite Absalom's act of rebellion and treachery, David loved his son as he loved himself. He was overcome with grief and went into his private chamber where he lamented, "O my son Absalom! My son, my son Absalom! If only I had died instead of you—O Absalom, my son, my son!" (2 Samuel 18:33).

The final step of contemplation and intimacy is compassion. We may go through the first nine steps to intimacy only to fail at the last, that of compassion. When we begin to understand the dynamics of our pain and who has hurt us, it is easy to turn on those responsible and seek vengeance. A lack of compassion towards those who have hurt us can generate enormous anger and resentment. True healing means being willing to say to the parent, husband, wife, child, or friend who hurt you: "I forgive you, and I still love you." Sometimes we need to say this to ourselves.

David's soldiers could not understand his grief. After all, the rebellion was now over and the treacherous Absalom was dead. Joab castigated him for showing remorse over the very one who had betrayed him and caused such turmoil in the kingdom. But he did not understand the powerful sense of intimacy that allowed David to weep for the one who hurt him. David's love for Absalom was such that he had no choice but to grieve deeply for him.

Compassion is the test of contemplation and intimacy. Are we compassionate towards ourselves, our neighbors, the world, and God?

Contemplation manifests itself in the depth of compassion, allowing our capacity for intimacy to be seen in the little things. What is our response when someone makes a mistake that causes us a minor headache? Do we feel anger and self-righteous indignation, or do we see ourselves in the faults of others and feel the same compassion we would desire to have others show us? Perhaps we feel both, and can learn to act on the compassion.

CONCLUSION

Contemplation is like the water of a pond. When the waters are stirred by strong winds there is no clarity; the bottom cannot be seen. But as calmness settles over the pond, the water becomes transparent and the bottom can be seen clearly. The same clarity and stillness comes to our lives in contemplation and is manifested in compassion, opening us up to intimacy with God and sweeping away false expectations of ourselves and others.

The story is told of a little boy who lived in a camp on the shores of the Mississippi River. One day as he was sitting with a hobo, or drifter, on the riverbank a big steamboat came into view. The little boy called out, "Come over here!" The hobo laughed. "Don't waste your time. That boat has better things to do than come over here and see you!"

But the boy persisted, and to the hobo's surprise, the steamboat started moving towards where the boy was standing. The *hobo* watched with amazement as the huge boat pulled up to the bank and lowered its gangplank. As the young boy climbed aboard he turned to the hobo and said, "I told you it would come. You see, the Captain is my daddy."

Contemplation means life has a Captain, who is our Heavenly Father, the head of the ship that is our life. We may not be able to bring back a relationship that we have lost—to which we entrusted our meaning and value as a human being—but we can open ourselves to His love, which melts away our false selves and then brings healing to the hurt, dark, and destroyed parts of our lives.

His love transforms the chaos of our inner selves and gives us "beauty instead of ashes" (Isaiah 61:3). May God's love help us as we move towards contemplation and intimacy so that, like the little boy, we will realize: "It'll come, because the Captain is my daddy."

Our Father in heaven,
hallowed be your name,
your kingdom come,
your will be done
on earth as it is in heaven (Matthew 6:9-13).

CHAPTER 9
MARY MAGDALENE: FROM WOUNDS TO WORSHIP

New life is born in the state of total vulnerability - this is the mystery of love.
Power kills. Weakness creates. It creates autonomy, self awareness, and freedom.
(Henri Nouwen[1])

THE MARYS OF THIS WORLD

Since 1980 my major work and study has focused on the dynamics of
cocaine, particularly crack addiction. This work has taken me through the
perils of drug addiction in Europe, the Bahamas, the Caribbean, the U.S.A.
and South America. During this time I have been deeply involved with
many women I think of as *the Mary Magdalene type*. In the drug world of
the Caribbean the women drug pushers and couriers are called *babbits*.
These women are hard and tough; they control the cocaine and are often
feared by the men. The babbits are very hurt women, many have been
abused, but they are also very strong and play a major role in the drug
camps (broken houses or spaces in the woods where people gather to use
drugs). They are able to manipulate the other addicts because they always
have a supply of drugs, but this life is dangerous and many of them are

beaten or even killed. In working with them, if they accept you, they form a very deep alliance and without their help my own particular work would not have been possible.

One of the women who was particularly involved in my work was an attractive young lady whom I will call Doreen. Originally from America, she ended up in the Bahamas where she became a severe cocaine addict and pusher. I met her in hospital where she was recovering from a serious gunshot wound. During my rounds, she shared with me the perils of living a babbit's life, "Dr. Allen I have done so much evil. The cocaine world is a dirty world; I would like to stop and get out, but I can't." After leaving hospital, she would come to my office and many times steal something. I remember one time watching her walk out of the office with my clock. When challenged she said, "I was only borrowing it." In spite of my efforts to treat her with respect, she still stole from me. Sometimes she and her gang would steal the battery from my car. I tried to admit her to the state hospital and to involve her with my outpatient program, but she refused both of them. I failed miserably in my attempts to help her.

One day I was particularly exasperated because she stole my briefcase full of research papers. Meeting her, I pleaded for the return of the papers, as they would be difficult to replace. Eventually she said, "Okay, let's go in your car." She directed me through some back streets and interesting small lanes until we came to a broken-down house, where she shouted, "Boys, bring Dr. Allen's briefcase." And sure enough, after a while, a little guy emerged with my briefcase and gave it to me.

On another occasion my secretary said, "Dr. Allen, there's a posh English lady on the phone." Picking up the phone, I inquired who it was and a familiar voice said, "Dr. Allen, this is no English lady, this is Doreen. I have been locked up by the police and I told them that you and I are doing research on cocaine and so I hope they'll let me out." That afternoon she appeared in my office saying that she had been released to continue her research! In certain cocaine camps, particular areas where it was very dangerous to go, Doreen would escort me by night and day. She gave me many insights into the dangers of cocaine—I learnt much from her. But I always felt a sense of pathos in the pain and chaos of her life.

Becoming pregnant, Doreen continued to use cocaine and at the time of delivery I visited her and the baby in hospital. Doreen shared with me that just after the baby was born, she had a severe craving for cocaine and jumped out of the hospital window, had a hit of cocaine and returned. After she left hospital I met her, with her little baby, while doing rounds in a community-based cocaine treatment program. She said, "Dr. Allen, the baby was crying last night and I couldn't get her to stop, so I let her take a whiff of my cocaine and she calmed down right away." Hopeless and horrifying, her story indicates the bizarreness, degradation, and dehumanization of the cocaine saga. On another occasion while visiting Washington on business, I called my Nassau office only to have Doreen answer the phone. Shocked and terrified I said in my heart, "Lord, into your hands I commit my office and all that I possess." After catching myself I asked, "Doreen what are you doing in my office?" She replied, "Your secretary went to the bathroom, and so I thought I'd help out."

When I saw Doreen a few years later she was eating out of a dustbin. I had failed miserably to make a difference—failed miserably to impact her addiction. What a hopeless sight. The feeling in my heart was one of total failure.

These are just a few glimpses of my experience with someone who was rather like Mary Magdalene. The Marys of this world are loving, kind, and committed. Beneath the painful and abused facade, there is a beautiful person looking for meaning, connection, and community.

CONTEMPLATION IN MARY'S LIFE

Tradition has it that Mary Magdalene was a deeply troubled woman who led a reprobate and destructive life. Some say she was known as a prostitute, but people argue that there is no evidence for this, although the town of Magdala was known for its prostitution. The beautiful painting by the French artist Georges de la Tour portrays the simplicity, profundity and grief of this interesting lady. According to St. Luke's gospel, Mary Magdalene was exorcised of seven demons (Luke 8:2). From my travels and work in many parts of the world, including the Caribbean and South America, my understanding of demon possession is that it often indicates that a person has been severely abused and deeply hurt. Whatever her way of life, we know that Mary Magdalene was a deeply hurt, perhaps sexually abused woman who found it very difficult to put life together. She found herself turning away from the positive force of life to open herself to the darker, sinister forces of life. Mary's experience, whatever it was, was probably very hard, and would have led to the hardening of her heart and given her a tough attitude to life.

Connection

Mary Magdalene met our Lord and the connection was very powerful. She saw in Jesus a person who cared for her, understood her pain, and was willing to forgive her. This is always a tremendous blessing to someone who lives under a load of guilt, rejecting themselves and feeling people do not care about them. When Mary Magdalene met Jesus, I think she saw the look in his eyes and the tenderness of his face, felt the compassion of his touch, and she opened her heart to him. Made in the image of God, human beings all have a longing for God. Mary Magdalene, despite her experience, had a deep longing for God and when she met Christ, she found in him a new peace, a new hope. Human beings, regardless of how debased or fallen, have a sincere desire to see the face of God because we are made in his image. Seeing the face of Christ and interacting with him made Mary Magdalene want to open to the love that would not let her go and the face that would never turn away.

Being in the image of God, in our highest state we are reflectors of God—the good, the true, and the beautiful. But life is wounded and whether we call it sin, pathological narcissism, or using Freud's term the ambivalence between Eros (life force) and Thanatos (death force), we human beings suffer alienation from God, ourselves, each other, and nature. The brain, in order to cope with this woundedness in our lives, creates a false self to defend against the pain. From the perspective of child development discussed previously (chapters 4 and 6), the child has at least three basic needs: survival-security—how will I survive, how secure will I be; affection-esteem—who will love me and how will I feel about myself; power-control—will I have some autonomy over my life? All of us, in some way, have been hurt in each of these areas. The deprivation in these instinctual needs creates abandonment, rejection, and humiliation or shame issues. No doubt Mary Magdalene was hurt in all three areas. She knew the meaning of being abandoned, rejected, and shamed. This red-hot figurative triangle of abandonment, rejection, and humiliation is the hurt trail that characterizes so many of our inner lives. Mary Magdalene, no doubt, had a very powerful hurt trail.

In Mary Magdalene's life, losses and grief had produced a state of alienation from herself and others in the world. It was in her state of pain—abandonment, rejection, and shame—that she encountered the Christ. Experiencing a meaningful, empathic connection with Jesus she felt loved and cared for in a special way. As a result, the light of healing shone in her heart and she committed herself to the one whose love she always sought, for in Christ she saw the face of God. Looking at her, Christ loved her and had compassion for her, melting away the false self to open her to her true self in God. This takes place with much anxiety because the false self, like an onion with many coverings, covers up our true selves in God. But only true love, the unconditional love of God, can reduce the influence of the false self. Eckhart Tolle talks about the importance of being attached to the Eternal Being—the one who is ineffable, eternal, and infinite.[2] As we open to the Eternal Being and surrender our lives, we experience the eternal light that reveals things we could not see in our so-called impure state. Encountering Jesus, Mary Magdalene was seen not as a reprobate or a failure, but as someone made in the image of the loving God, who was calling her. This internal transformation coming from the connection with Christ had a powerful effect on her life. Jesus said, "If anyone would come after me, he must deny himself [that is his false self] and take up his cross [face his pain] and follow me" (Mark 8:34). Mary, upon encountering Christ, let go of her false self and opened to God who revealed her true self in love.

Being a mystic, Mary Magdalene had an intense realization of God within herself while she herself was embraced within God. In mysticism there is deep darkness, the darkness of not knowing, and there is light, with flashes, in which the self knows the unknowable to be terribly near and know itself as never before.

Silence

All this happens in silence. As Jesus met Mary the concept of contemplation or the transformation of consciousness happened in silence. "Be still and know that I am God" (Psalm 46:10). "In quietness and trust is your strength" (Isaiah 30:15). Silence opens us to the presence of God. Exterior silence leads to interior silence and that produces a powerful stillness, a stillness associated with space, space where God can meet us, God can touch us, God can heal us. Georges de la Tour's painting of Mary

Magdalene overwhelms me with a sense of silence and quiet. I see a lady whose contemplative spirit projects a powerful sense of silence, silence that speaks so loudly that I want to listen to her, and hear what is happening in her life. In the stillness produced by interior silence, there is a table set for two, God and us. The encounter between Mary and Jesus led to a deep, deep relationship where Christ was able to meet her at the inner table of her person, sheltered and protected by God's presence and love. In communion with him, we too come as new people basking in the love of Christ. Contemplation means learning to be silent, it means stopping and listening to the silence, to all the sounds and spaces that give shape to our lives. "In repentance and rest is your salvation, in quietness and trust is your strength" (Isaiah 30:15). Or as Michael Ramsey said,

> Be where you are. Look around.
> Just look, don't interpret.
> See the light, colors, textures.
> Be aware of the silent presence of each thing
> ...Listen to the sounds, don't judge them
> Listen to the silence under the sounds.[3]

In our busy lives we hurt ourselves by not stopping, looking, and listening. God was not in the earthquake; he was not in the lightening or the thunder. He was in the still, calm breeze, bathing and soothing Elijah, eliminating his negativity and renewing his faith (1 Kings 19:11-13). Mary Magdalene was changed by her contact with Christ, but this change was not outward, it was internal. It was a change of the heart. It was a change that involved knowing beyond knowing. It was a change ordained by God himself. It was rational, yet beyond rationality. It was a change of faith.

Commitment

In relationships we all enjoy the attractive phase where we feel deeply connected to our loved ones. As attraction deepens and fusion occurs, our ego boundaries break down and we feel a sense of ecstasy. Commitment is easy when things are going our way. But fusion never lasts forever; the crisis will come. When the crisis comes, things change, and we tend to withdraw and seek cover behind our various defenses. But crisis is the acid test of commitment. After following Christ so closely, Mary experienced the crisis of his crucifixion. His disciples had all run away and hidden and the situation looked dark and hopeless. Committed, Mary Magdalene stayed at the cross with Mary the mother of Jesus. I think her commitment said, "I met a man who gave me a new life, allowed me to touch who I really am, and represents where I wish to go. I've seen the face that never turns away and experienced the love that will not let me go! This was no ordinary man or happening. I will stay with him even in death, at his crucifixion." What a deep sense of commitment!

So often the missing link in our spiritual journey is a simple, open commitment to follow God wherever he leads. Like the disciples, Mary no doubt felt fear, the passion of grief, maybe anger at the way Christ was treated, and even anger at being left by him. But the most beautiful thing is that she stayed there. Commitment really means learning to stay there. If we are going to heal the pain in our hearts, we have to stay there; if we are going to open to God's grace in our life, we have to stay there. This is easier said than done. After Christ was buried, the next day certainly must have been a long day with question after question. But the hunch in Mary's heart was that this was not the end. Faith has its own way of speaking to us, and so, early on the first day of the week while it was still dark, Mary traveled alone to the tomb seeking the Lord who blessed her so much (John 20:1). This is deep commitment!

Community

One of the characteristics of our Lord's life on earth is that he established a community who traveled with him and supported his ministry. Mary Magdalene was a key part of that community and was very close to Jesus and the other disciples. Sadly, the arrest and crucifixion of Christ led to a fragmentation of the community as they all ran to seek safety in hiding. But Mary Magdalene was different. She had the courage to venture forth in search of the Love that changed her life, regardless of the dangers awaiting her. This is a beautiful picture of community, but it also reminds us that community is not uniform—some will still stay together in spite of circumstances while others are fair-weather friends, who disappear when the going gets tough!

When Mary arrived at the tomb, the angels told her that Jesus was raised. He was not dead (Matthew 28:5-6). Shocked and surprised, Mary could have stayed there and basked in her amazement, but being a part of the community she ran to tell the rest of the disciples the good news. We can only imagine what it was like for the disciples, who were hiding in fear, to hear Mary's news. Extremely excited, they ran with her to the tomb. Recognizing that Jesus was not there, they were afraid that they would be blamed for stealing his body. Terrified, they retreated in fear to their hiding place. Fear has a paralyzing effect on us all—it destroys contemplation, undermines faith, and causes us to move away from our true selves in God and worship at the dictates of our false, defensive selves. Contemplation means hearing afresh the words of God. "So do not fear, for I am with you" (Isaiah 41:10).

Persistence

Returning home is where business is as usual and we feel safe. When we face difficult times, when life seems hard and things don't work out, or go our way, many of us tend to give in and to go back home. Returning to the old way of doing things, we hide in our comfort zones. But Mary Magdalene persisted; she stayed there (John 20:10-11). Staying there is not easy. Healing requires staying there. Contemplation means staying there, doing our daily Lectio Devina and silent prayer, and moving into action. This requires persistence and yet more persistence. It is not easy for us and was not easy for Mary. Grief had over taken her heart, and she was crying profusely. Asked why was she crying, she said, "They have taken my Lord away" (John 20:13-14). He was the person who gave her a sense of meaning, the person who changed her life, the person who gave her hope for the first time. Life had become perilous; she was seeing the shadow side of God. But she stayed there, she was persistent. Mary stayed there alone. She experienced the pain of separation that leads to growth.

Sometimes our spiritual journey is lonely. The crowd will not come with us. We have to stand alone as Mary did. Often contemplation calls us to be alone with God. Know that God has separated the Godly person for himself (Psalm 4:3). Contemplation requires persistence because it's all about waking up to be fully present where we are. As Ronald Rolheiser says, "We are in contemplation when we stand before reality and experience it just as it is."[4]

Grief

In her aloneness, Mary grieved the loss of what could have been—the loss of that closeness with him, the loss of the love she felt so deeply for him, the loss of a future that had seemed so certain. Most of all Mary probably grieved that it had ended this way—how could it when she had a hunch in her heart that there was more? Mary was crying (John 20:11). Grieving is the hallmark of someone living a contemplative lifestyle who, recognizing the presence of God in the world, is appalled by the pain of life, the suffering of children, the carnage of war, and the unfairness that governs our society. We cannot but grieve and wish our Lord were present, we miss him deeply. Have you missed the Lord? Have you ever stopped to say, "I wish you here"? Or, "I wish you would explain what's going on"? But this is our lot, this side of heaven. We have to be content with what it means to grieve, because life is not fair and many times is beyond our grasp. Despite this, our vocation is to remain faithful and make our contribution where we are, however little it might be. According to Henri Nouwen, "Grieving is praying. But grief is the discipline of the heart that sees the sin of the world, and knows itself to be the sorrowing price of freedom without which love cannot bloom."[5]

Surrender

Mary had to let go. She had to let go of her desire for safety. She had to let go of her desire to change the situation. She had to let go of her wish that Christ had not been crucified. She had to surrender! She could no longer control her security. But as we surrender and open ourselves to the Eternal Being, the lights go on! And so, in a very deep sense surrender is not fatalism. Surrender is opening to say to our Lord, "Yet not what I will, but what you will" (Mark 14:36). Surrender is saying, "Lord, I can no longer do it, you have to do it." Surrender is not taking the easy option, but allowing ourselves to be still and prepared to do what we have to do. But more than this, surrender is opening to God's presence, admitting our failures and shortcomings, and allowing him to direct us.

Mary was crying and distraught; by missing God she showed how close she was to him. Often God's presence is made real to us in his absence. After all, we can only miss that which we know. Learning to see with the eyes of her heart, Mary missed our Lord, but her desire for him increased. Seeing Christ in the garden, she mistook him for a gardener. After all, it is only common sense that the man in the garden early in the morning must be a gardener. In the same way, a child seeing a dog is told the dog has four legs, a pointed face, and a tail. When the child sees a cow he says, "big dog," because he recognizes the cow has four legs, a pointed face, and a tail. But if the child is to grow, he must develop a new schema for cow, one that is different from dog.

So often in our lives we are addicted to the schema of the familiar: we say that the man in the garden must be the gardener. And we therefore do not see the presence of Christ. Only as we are willing to be alone, to separate and individuate, will our eyes be opened to see God. The man in the garden is no longer the gardener but Christ himself. God the lover always reaches out to the beloved, and Mary heard Christ call to her. The blessing of individuation was manifested in the separation, loneliness, and isolation as Christ called to her saying, "Mary," and she replied, "Teacher" (John 20:16). Experiencing the vision of God, she ran up to him, she held him, she clung to him, she did not want to let him go. Christ tenderly said, "Do not hold on to me" and ordered her to the mission of going and telling his brothers (John 20:17). She had the vision of God's presence, God's love. She was the first to know that Christ had risen from the dead. But the vision must be matched with the mission. Christ asked her not to hold him, but to go and tell his brothers that he was alive, that the one who was dead had risen. Does God have a sense of humor? The first to know the true meaning of life, the meaning of the resurrection, was not a theologian, not a politician, but a lady who had been demon possessed and abused.

TOWARDS A DEFINITION OF CONTEMPLATION

Contemplation is derived from the word template, which means measurement. In the early Roman Empire, the augurs (the wise men) would make measurements on the earth to correspond to the templates in the heavens. Thus contemplation means living our life from the heavenly perspective. It is recognition that we are the temple of God—we are God's home

(1 Corinthians 3:16). Contemplation is the process that involves the transformation of consciousness so that God's love is the motivating force of our total existence. It involves a two-level perspective. First, there is the vision of God, "Holy, holy, holy is the Lord Almighty" (Isaiah 6:3); second, there is the mission of God's love, the living out of God's love in the world, "The whole earth is full of his glory" (Isaiah 6:3). The vision of God without the accompanying mission of God's love creates an empty hallucination or an otherworldly sentimental philosophy. The mission of God's love without the vision of God ends up as sanctified busyness and non-redemptive anxiety. The vision and the mission must go hand-in-hand. Moses was called to the mountaintop to experience the vision of God, which meant coming apart to wait in silence. But the test of true contemplation was that Moses came down from the mountain and continued to represent the mission of God's love in the world among the people.

The angels announcing the birth of Christ said, "Glory to God in the highest [the vision], and on earth peace to men on whom his favor rests [the mission]" (Luke 2:14). Contemplation involves these two components. In active contemplation we involve ourselves in the practice of contemplative prayer and wait for God, but there is also a passive element where we open ourselves in faith. God, in turn, gives us the grace to experience the inner peace and joy resulting from the union of his spirit with our spirit. Active contemplation is definitely our commitment. Passive contemplation depends on God's will. In my own experience, I feel that whenever we center in God with the intention of consenting to his presence and action in our lives and the world, through the mystery of the Holy Spirit, contemplative prayer results. This happens whether we are conscious of it or not because, "The Spirit himself testifies with our spirit that we are God's children" (Romans 8:16). Categorically, God says that if we draw near to him, he will in turn draw near to us (Psalm 145:18).

In the truest sense, Mary was a deep contemplative—she stood with the crucified Lord and faced fear and persecution and the pathos of his suffering. Connected deeply to him, she went to the tomb on Easter morning while it was still dark, facing the harsh reality of loss. As she persisted at the empty tomb, the Lord in her heart was revealed to her in external reality—and in an escalating cadence she was catapulted into the mystery and reality of the victory over death, so that life rejoiced with hope and flowed with a new harmony— she experienced intimacy in a distant world.

CONCLUSION

On Christmas Eve 2001, as I was driving along Bay Street in Nassau, a very neatly dressed lady shouted out to me, "Dr. Allen!" I stopped to see who it was and, because of the heavy traffic, I invited her into the car. To my surprise it was Doreen. She told me she hadn't used cocaine for the past two years and was now married and working in a jewelry store. She had come to faith in Christ and her life had changed. Shocked? I was amazed! How could this be? She was supposed to be a failure. In the silence it was as if God reminded me, "David, you are not in charge. I am! What you consider hopeless does not mean hopeless. Remember I am in charge. I am the source of all hope, all faith. Merry Christmas."

This was a special Christmas gift to me. As Doreen left the car to return to work, I found myself still stopped in traffic, wondering and pondering. I reminded myself of the Virgin Mary who, when she received the witness of God, pondered these things in her heart. Doreen's life, which in some sense represented my total failure and hopelessness, opened me to the healing grace of God. In my failure, my limitation, faith takes over and Doreen is changed. How important it is for us to realize that we are not in charge. But letting go is easier said than done. We have to surrender. God raises up and God puts down, salvation belongs to him and him alone. All we can do is bow in obedience to him, trusting him and his grace. There will be times of failure, of hopelessness, of extreme emptiness, but the light of his grace breaks through the darkness of life. For in his light we see light; he alone is the fountain of life.

REFERENCES

1. Henri Nouwen, *Intimacy* (New York: Harper and Row, 1969), 32.
2. Eckhart Tolle, *Practicing the Power of Now*, (Novato, California: New World Library, 2001), 112.
3. Michael Ramsey, in *Through the Year with Michael Ramsey,* ed. Margaret Duggan (London: Hodder and Stoughton; 1975), 164.
4. Ronald Rolheiser, *The Shattered Lantern* (New York: Crossroad

Publishing Co., 2001), 23.

5. Henri Nouwen, *The Return of the Prodigal Son: A Story of Homecoming* (New York: Doubleday, 1994), 129.

CHAPTER 10
RUTH AND NAOMI: LOVING WHEN
THE DREAM IS SHATTERED

Love is patient, love is kind...it always protects, always trusts, always hopes, always perseveres. (1 Corinthians 13:4,7)

Dreams and longings are a part of being human. Central to our passions and imagination, they become a part of our hearts. Sadly, when they shatter they leave our hearts broken. This is particularly true of the dream of love; a shattered dream of love is one of the strongest resistances to loving. Where we expected love, we received pain and as a result we fear love because it may cause pain. Mrs. Jones was happily married—life was beautiful. Then Mr. Jones told her that he was leaving the marriage for a new love. The shock and pain crushed her. Life became dark and terrible. "When my husband left me, I kept on performing but I stopped living. You see me in church, but I am not there. You see me at work, but much of me is missing; my world has collapsed."

Dreams or goals for the future have to be appropriate. A dream of childhood, if not reassessed, can create much pain in adult life. As one lady said, "When I grew up I wanted to have a special kind of husband, live in a sophisticated neighborhood, be well off and have children who were outstanding in their achievements. But," she reflected, "forty years later, things have not turned out that way. I have an ordinary husband, I live in a lower middle class neighborhood, I'm struggling financially, and my children have not been particularly successful." And as she tells her story, the pain, hurt, and disappointment are obvious. As life proceeds we have to adjust our dreams or we will find that they are destroying us. Speaking of a dream deferred, Langston Hughes wrote:

What happens to a dream deferred?

Does it dry up
like a raisin in the sun?

Or fester like a sore—
and then run?

Does it stink like rotten meat?
Or crust and sugar over—
like a syrupy sweet?

Maybe it just sags
like a heavy load.

Or does it just explode? [1]

Our hopes and dreams always have deep psychological significance. All humans have basic instinctual needs: Survival-security, will I survive or how secure will I be? Affection-esteem, who will love me and how will I value myself? Power-control, will I have some autonomy over my life? But life is wounded and all of us, in one way or another, are deprived in one or more of these instinctual needs (chapter 3). As a result, we suffer from abandonment, rejection, and humiliation. But wherever there is deprivation, the brain seeks to compensate. In essence then, our dreams are often compensations for our feelings of inadequacy. For example, a poor boy dreams of being a rich man. Many times, the deeper the inadequacy, the greater the dream will be. When a dream is purely a defense against our childhood trauma, we may not lay the proper foundations to fulfill the dream, and as we get older it collapses. There was a gentleman who said that he wanted to be the Prime Minister of Germany before he was fifty, but at forty-nine years old he had not even entered politics. Obviously, he needed to let that dream go.

We often forget that a dream shattered is similar to a dream achieved. A dream shattered is finished and we need a new dream. Similarly a dream achieved is also finished and we must find a new one. In a special sense all dreams are a longing: a longing for our deeper selves, a longing for love— the good, the true, and the beautiful, a longing for God, the love that will never let us go and the face that never turns away.

> How lovely is your dwelling place,
> O Lord Almighty!
> My soul yearns, even faints,
> for the courts of the Lord ;
> my heart and my flesh cry out
> for the living God (Psalm 84:1-2).

The age-old question is, how does one love when the dream of love is shattered? The shattering of the dream of love is holy ground—for there is no more sacred and holy experience than this in a human being's life. To discuss the issue I have chosen to reflect on the ancient Jewish story of Ruth and Naomi, a simple but deeply profound story that has nurtured my heart during times of pain and crisis. This classic story is old yet ever new, a story for all times. It speaks the language of our hearts, it is our experience.

FINDING NO BREAD

Naomi and her husband Elimelech lived in the ancient town of Bethlehem. Apparently Bethlehem means the place of bread. But as the story goes, there was a famine in the land; there was no bread in the so-called place of bread. Sometimes where we expect hope, we find despair; where we expect light, we find darkness; where we expect joy, we find unhappiness. For example, the job was supposed to be a place of bread, but it was not. Our life was supposed to be nurtured by the bread of hope and love—but as time went on we came up empty, there was no bread. We joined a church to find a spirituality that would feed our souls and provide manna from heaven—but the sermons were dry, the people distant, and love had grown cold. There was no bread. We married looking for nurture and sustenance from each other, but then as the years passed, our hopes faded. It started off so beautifully, and then there was no bread. George said that his home used to be so wonderful, a place of joy, excitement, and happiness. Then tragedy struck—Dad died and things changed. Home now is so cold he could ice-skate from the living room to the kitchen. There is no bread. Dreaming of a tremendous career, a young man started out with enthusiasm and excitement. Working very hard, he started to advance, but then something happened and the company went bankrupt. Losing his job, he just couldn't get on his feet again. Sadly, in the place where he expected bread, there was no bread. This is always a painful experience. I'm sure if we think back over our lives, we can all describe experiences where we expected bread, but came up empty.

GOING TO MOAB

Recognizing that things were tough in Bethlehem, Elimelech decided to take his family to Moab. During the early days of the Judges immediately preceding the events in our story, Moab had enslaved the children of Israel (Judges 3:12-14). The Moabites were the enemy of Israel. It was hard to leave aristocracy in Bethlehem to become a sharecropper in Moab. It was a tough life but when human beings face pain, expedience becomes the norm. Facing the hurt and pains of life, many of us choose our different Moabs—sexuality, pornography, workaholism, drug abuse, materialism, power, control, etc. Human beings will do almost anything to defend against pain. Remember Abraham had been called by God to leave his home in Ur of the Chaldeans, to journey to Canaan (Genesis 11:31). Obeying the sovereignty of God, Abraham journeyed in faith.

Arriving in Canaan he established the altar where he called upon God and pitched his tent, a reminder that life is transitory. But there was a famine in Canaan, so there was no food or water for his animals. In other words, in the place where he expected bread, there was no bread. And even though he was not supposed to go to Egypt, because of his feelings of abandonment, rejection, and humiliation, Abraham, the Godly patriarch, ignored his spiritual directions and followed the dictates of his false self.

Asking his wife Sarah to act as his sister, he lied to the Pharaoh and gave Sarah to the king's harem to protect his own skin and make him rich (chapter 7). When our backs are against the wall, it's amazing what we will do. Pain makes desperates of us all, causing us to choose our Moabs.

In Moab life was very difficult for Elimelech. He was under a lot of stress, working hard to provide for his family, and he died. Later on his two sons, who were married to the Moabite women Ruth and Orpah, also died (Ruth 1:3-5). Bereaved, poor, and hopeless, Naomi was left alone with her widowed daughters-in-law. The dream of love had been shattered.

FACING SHATTERED DREAMS

In this simple but ancient story, we have a few principles that may act as a guide and help us understand how to face the shattering of the dream of love in our own lives. There is no simple formula or panacea, for every experience is individual and different, but we can glean principles from the lives of God's people.

Accept reality

So often when our dreams of love are shattered, we are afraid to face reality. We deny it and sometimes try to reconstruct it, but not face it. Other times we project our problems on others, blaming them, and not taking responsibility. Or we are harsh on ourselves and become masochistic, punishing ourselves severely. It is so important to surrender to reality as it is, and not as we would like it to be. So often when we go through the shattering of the dream of love we get caught in a past-future prison. The past loss is so painful that it projects negative pictures on the screen of the future so that we spend our life living in the past-future prison and as a result lose our ability to act in the present. According to Eckhart Tolle, author of The Power of Now,

> To the ego, the present moment hardly exists, only past and future are considered important. This total reversal of truth accounts for the fact that in the ego mode, the mind is so dysfunctional. It is always concerned with keeping the past alive, because without it – who are you? It

constantly projects itself into the future to ensure its
continued survival and seeks some kind of release
or fulfillment there.[2]

Surrender means opening up to hurt, tragedy, and loss, we then are
able to be open to the present. The presence of God's love and hope is
always in the present. Because of this, living in the present fortifies us in
God's love—giving us courage to face the reality of negativity, hurt, pain,
and fear. Sadly, many of us are terrified of the fear of helplessness, making
it difficult to acknowledge our helplessness, without which we are unable
to seek or accept help. Naomi accepted that things were tough. Her husband and children were dead, and she was a poor hopeless widow, with
no future to offer her daughters-in-law. Her dream of love was shattered.
But even in our darkest period, surrendering to God and accepting our
situation allows hope to spring and grow. It is like our life is in a fog, but
surrendering opens us to the unchanging Eternal Being, and in the midst
of the fog a light goes on, enabling us to see the next step. Often we get
discouraged because we cannot see the whole way ahead, but it helps to
realize that the light of acceptance often reveals only the next step, and
we must walk in faith. There can be no healing unless we honestly accept
the reality of the shattered dream of love. This may sound simple, but in
my experience it is one of the hardest things.

Open to community

When a dream of love is shattered it is important to open up to the
communities of our lives. This is no time to try and develop community;
this has to be done in the good times. So often we wait until our dream of
love is shattered before we seek to develop community but the time to put
effort into building community is when things are going well and we have
emotional resources to spare. This may involve organizing simple dinners
or lunches, having a time of prayer with a particular person, writing a letter, making an important call or helping somebody in crisis.

Recognizing that her dream of love had been shattered, Naomi called
together her existing community, which included her two daughters-in-law
Orpah and Ruth (Ruth 1:7-8). It can be hard to be part of a community in
pain and so we tend to avoid or disconnect from each other during times

of great trial. It requires a special effort to involve ourselves with persons who are experiencing hurt and loss so that we can support them. For example, when Absalom displaced his father David from the throne, David sought solace in his community, the people around him who were willing to stick with him in good and bad times (chapter 8). Community is important because even though pain can be very difficult and very hard to cope with, community allows us to share the burden, making it just a bit more bearable. The life of our Lord, who chose twelve disciples to be his close friends before he started his early ministry, also demonstrates this. Among that twelve were three—Peter, James, and John—who were even closer to him. His community also included close relationships with women— Martha and Mary of Bethany and Mary Magdalene and others who supported him financially (Luke 10:38-39; Mark 15:40). When Jesus went to the Garden of Gethsemane on the night he was betrayed, he asked three disciples to go with him (Mark 14:33). This is community.

True community also requires meaningful solitude. In other words, if we cannot be alone in a meaningful way, it is difficult to be together in communion. Without solitude, we are unable to be nurtured by the presence of God's love and instead we will experience loneliness when alone. A group of lonely people does not form community, but a crowd. One of the difficulties in modern culture is that we have lost the gift of solitude and hence the cultivation of meaningful communion. Bonded to her daughters-in-law, Naomi described the situation accurately. They knew what was going on. They acknowledged that Naomi had lost her husband. They acknowledged that they had lost their husbands. They knew that things were very, very difficult (Ruth 1:11-14). As a result there was no denial, rejection, projection or displacement, but the bare naked acceptance of the reality that they were three desperate, hurting women who were bonded together in community. In modern culture it is often hard to find this depth of community. The real tragedy is that many of us have no community and therefore experience the shattered dream of love in isolation without support and love. In light of this, a revolution in the church is the formation of small groups to enhance intimacy bonding, which in turn helps the church to develop into a more caring and empathic community.

Recognize God's providence

When our dreams of love are shattered, in a very deep sense our hearts are broken. Facing the pain deep in our hearts purifies our longings. We long for somebody to love us and to be close to us. But in essence this is really a longing for the love that will not let us go and the face that will not turn away. It is a longing for God. As painful as the loss or shattering of the dream of love may be, it cannot alter God's love and sovereignty. His love is eternal, ineffable, and ever continuing. In the organization Alcoholics Anonymous, when members realize that their lives are unmanageable, they recognize the need for a power or source of energy greater than themselves. To cope with the shattered dream of love, we must recognize our shattered dreams before the eternal God who is unchanging and eternal. In a changing world, faith and trust in the Almighty is an unchanging core and point of stability.

Speaking with passion in her voice, Naomi told her young daughters-in-law, "May the Lord show kindness to you, as you have shown to your dead and to me" (Ruth 1:8). Recognizing God's providence in spite of her hurt and despair, Naomi thanked them for their kindness and invoked the blessing of God upon them. Prayer, particularly in a time of crisis, reveals the state of our hearts. Thus her prayer and appreciation of the kindness of her daughters-in-law demonstrated a grateful heart. Feeling terrible, Naomi knew that the future would be bleak and hopeless, but in spite of this, her faith shone through as she expressed a deep sense of gratitude.

Kindness and gratitude demonstrated that Naomi had not let her heart become hardened by her pain. This is not easy. Life involves change, change involves loss, and all loss involves pain. But at the point of our pain, we can make a choice. We can become angry, bitter, and vindictive and let our hearts become hardened, or we can do the grief work to move our hearts to gratitude. Perhaps most of us move a bit in both directions! A hardened heart is like a bucket of hard dry soil. When water is poured upon it, it settles on the top. Breaking up the soil is the only way to allow water to percolate through, and this is the only way a plant can grow in the soil. Doing our grief work is the only way to avoid a hardened heart. Meaningful community, where we are free to express a range of feelings such as gratitude, sadness, and hurt, becomes a powerful antidote to the hardening of the heart. When the dream of love is shattered, we can choose to face our pain, surrender it to God, and do the grief work.

When we lose love, there is grief or sadness about the loss, but there is also anger about losing the love. So often in our culture we stay at the anger pole because we feel it empowers us. The anger pole does empower us but it can prevent us from recognizing the love that exists around us. Healing our hearts requires a meaningful community to allow us to move from the anger pole to the grief pole. Yes, we experience sadness, but our hearts are emptied and open to the love around us. Even though we are still hurt, we can express gratitude and kindness, making growth and development possible, although the dream is shattered. As Tennyson said, "Tis better to have loved and lost than never to have loved at all."[3]

Be kind

Naomi's wish for her daughters-in-law was for them to experience kindness from God, similar to the kindness that they had shown her sons. So often when our hearts are hurt, it is easier to become cruel; hurt people tend to hurt themselves and those they love. Long-lasting, happy, stable relationships are characterized by kind initiatives. I do not mean a circumstantial happiness but the peace resulting from being anchored in our deeper selves in relationship with the eternal being. The daughters-in-law had been kind to their deceased husbands. So often what goes around comes around. Giving kindness prepares us to receive kindness. I will never forget a dear lady whose husband had abruptly left her for a new love, what he considered a more exciting and romantic experience. Despite her pain, she said, "I am very hurt, disappointed, and heartbroken, but I pray everyday to be kind. Because if I let myself ever become bitter and mean then I will be totally destroyed." When our dreams of love shatter, it is hard to be kind and open. We need to allow God's grace to enable us to be kind when we least feel like it.

Practice silence

Silence is the clearing house for much of the pain and hurt that we experience in our lives. As Henri Nouwen once said, "All healing words come from silence, are accompanied by silence, and go to silence."[4] Silence is one of the languages of God and when we are hurt, particularly when it involves the shattering of the dream of love, words can be inadequate to express the depth of feeling and hurt. The words in our souls remain inexpressible. As Ruth and the two younger women came together, beyond the words they shared and the tears they shed, there was a deep sense of silence. External silence creates interior silence, which creates a stillness and space for God; it creates a table set for two where God can sit with us. David, the ancient psalmist of Israel, said that he had learned to calm and quiet his heart because, "You prepare a table before me in the presence of my enemies" (Psalm 23:5). Silence empties our hearts because when the heart is still, the mind unloads the unconscious hurt and pain from all aspects of the body. Life is like a pond. When the pond is disturbed we cannot see the bottom, but as it settles we begin to see clearly. Silence allows the ponds of our lives to settle so that we can see things clearly. When we are hurt, it is hard to see things clearly, and as a result we may make unwise decisions, which are not in our best interests. At other times we can be very cruel and hurtful to others. Hurt, bereaved of their husbands, and grieving deeply, these women, in the midst of their sobs and tender words, expressed deep silence, a silence that spoke loudly, reminding them of their loss, hurt, and fears. This silence also speaks loudly to us, pointing beyond our own lives to a greater force that guides life. Let all the earth be silent, for the Lord is in his holy temple. "Be still and know that I am God" (Psalm 46:10). "In quietness and trust is your strength" (Isaiah 30:15).

Grieve

Naomi grieved deeply with her two daughters-in-law. The shattering of a dream is a terrible loss, and losses have a way of producing in us many different feelings; rage, anger, disorientation, depression, guilt, and shame all come together. Naomi and her daughters-in-law cried and shared their feelings. Because children can feel pain but find it difficult to grieve or process the pain, in some sense all of us have a lot of crying to do. Because the unaddressed pain of our early childhood experiences and losses in adult life are synergistic, when we open our hearts, grieving becomes the way of renewal. As Jesus said, "Blessed are those who mourn, for they will be comforted" (Matthew 5:4). Grieving reduces the power of our false selves, developed in early childhood to defend against our hurt feelings of abandonment, rejection, and humiliation. As we grieve the loss, we grieve the hurt of the present experience, but we also grieve the hurt experienced in our childhood, reducing the need for the defensive cover of our false selves. In other words, grieving opens us to our true selves, our deeper selves and God.

This may sound paradoxical in our culture, where being stoic and in control is the accepted way. But as we learn more about the inner life, we realize that only grieving can empty our hearts of hurt and pain. When the dream of love has been shattered, doing our grief work is the only way to heal our hearts. Sadly, when the dream of love shatters, often we deny reality, reject community, fill any silences with noise, and fail to do our grief work. As a result, we are condemned to aborted grief reactions defended by a powerful false self that promises relief but leads to further hurt. Defending us from our true selves, the false self creates an illusion in which we tend to hang onto experiences without substance, create relationships without depth, and move toward superficial living. This does not go on forever. At some time in our lives, the deep grief from hurts buried in our souls breaks through into our every-day lives, producing depression, rage, addiction and other destructive processes and filling our hearts with feelings of bitterness, shame, and guilt.

Naomi and her daughters-in-law grieved deeply. We can only grieve as deeply as we can love, and we can only love as deeply as we can grieve. And so Naomi and her daughters-in-law deeply expressed their love for each other in grief. Naomi was powerless and felt hopeless, but through her grief she was able to express herself. Loss always involves anger and pain, so grieving and anger are on the same continuum. Grieving always involves anger and sadness about the love lost. Positioning ourselves at the anger pole (discussed more fully in chapter 3) we feel empowered but cannot take advantage of the love that still exists. Whereas at the grieving pole, though we are sad we are able to open ourselves to the love and life around us.

Contemplation involves breaking up the unplowed ground of our hearts to let the water of God's love flow through. Grieving is not always shedding tears; it is confronting and being present to the hurt in our hearts. When grieving we should always ask, what is going on at this moment? As we observe our pain, we become present to and liberated from it. Grieving involves becoming conscious by facing the problem, accepting it, and dealing with it. Then a problem becomes a challenge and a challenge becomes an opportunity for us to address the situation. Often we may not solve the original problem, but in creating a challenge we create opportunities for growth. The sad thing is that sometimes when the dream of love is shattered, the loss is so powerful that without true grieving, it becomes organized and internalized as a part of our identity. When this occurs it creates a deep state of pain, which may stay with a person for a long time, sometimes a lifetime. As one lady said, "I loved once and was hurt. I will never let myself love again." Sadly her grief became organized and internalized, it became part of her identity, contaminating her life and preventing her from opening up to love that might be there for her.

Give others freedom

It was a bleak situation but Naomi confronted it head on. She was brutally honest with her daughters-in-law. She told them frankly that she had nothing to offer them. Her husband and her sons were dead, she was old and had no hope of having other children, and being a foreigner in a strange land, she had no network to provide for them. The bottom line was that things were tough and life was really hard. Unable to offer them any hope of a future, Naomi gave them their freedom, freedom to do exactly what they wanted to do, freedom to choose their own destinies. She encouraged them to return to their own culture (Ruth 1:8-11). This is beautiful, because so often when we are hurt, we cling to people, restricting their freedom and seeking to control them to meet our own needs, rather than seeking what is best for them. Naomi demonstrated a tremendous depth of character and maturity when, in the midst of pathos and pain, she gave her daughters-in-law the freedom to do whatever they wished.

The reaction of each daughter-in-law reflected the dynamics that occur so often in our hearts. Orpah, recognizing that the situation was hopeless, made a hasty exit to return to her people and her gods (Ruth 1:14-15). This finds resonance with the side of our own hearts that, upon confronting the painful reality of our hurt and the hopelessness of the situation, make haste to find cover or to return to the familiar. We should not blame Orpah in this situation because every human being has the right and freedom to make their own choice. She decided that the situation was so bleak and hopeless that the best thing to do was return to her people and find her faith there.

> One ship sails east
> And another west
> By the selfsame winds that blow;
> 'Tis the set of the sails
> And not the gales
> That tells them the way to go!

> Like the winds of the sea
> Are the waves of Time
> As we voyage along through life;
> 'Tis the set of the soul
> That determines the goal,
> And the not the calm or the strife. [5]

Ruth, on the other hand, looked beyond the painful situation to see the person of Naomi, her mother-in-law whom she had come to love and trust. Love is stronger than death and many waters cannot quench it. And so, in these beautiful words, Ruth begs Naomi not to send her away:

> Don't urge me to leave you or to turn back from you.
> Where you go I will go, and where you stay I will stay.
> Your people will be my people and your God my God.
> Where you die I will die, and there I will be buried. May
> the Lord deal with me, be it ever so severely, if anything
> but death separates you and me (Ruth 1:16,17).

What a beautiful statement of commitment. Even though Ruth had nothing to offer Naomi, she had a deep sense of commitment and offered herself. Walking back to Bethlehem, these two hurt, lonely, broken women had nothing to hang onto but friendship. There was nothing to hold onto but a sense of deep commitment to each other. There was nothing to look forward to but being together.

Be practical

When Naomi and Ruth returned to Bethlehem, Naomi's friends were shocked at her appearance (Ruth 1:19). Apparently Naomi means pleasant and in Bethlehem Naomi always appeared pleasant, happy, and comfortable. It is amazing how pain shows in our faces, and in Naomi's case hurt and grief had beaten her down. Responding to the dismay of her friends on seeing her, Naomi said, "Don't call me Naomi [pleasant], call me Mara [bitter], because the Almighty has made my life very bitter" (Ruth 1:20). In some sense she went out full but she came back empty. Pain has a powerful affect on our lives. Many of us can say the words of Naomi, "Don't call me Naomi, call me Mara, because the Almighty has made my life very bitter." Life at its heart is painful and as we face the ups and downs of our existence sometimes our bodies, minds, and hearts are forced through the pressure cooker of tribulation, suffering, and trial. Sometimes we cause our own suffering, but many times it is just a part of life.

Ruth and Naomi lived together in a harmonious relationship, and Naomi sought to counsel Ruth in the best way she knew how. To introduce Ruth to Bethlehem and its people, Naomi put Ruth in contact to her cousin Boaz, a wealthy farmer (Ruth 2:1). Boaz married Ruth and they had a child called Obed. Obed was the father of Jesse who was the father of David and out of David's lineage came our Lord Jesus Christ. The mystery of this all is that two lonely people, hurt and distraught though they were, in coming together created a sense of community out of which came the beautiful writings of the twenty-third Psalm, "The Lord is my shepherd, I shall not be in want" (Psalm 23:1). But most of all, in Ruth and Naomi's coming together, heaven came down and God himself sent his son, the Lord Jesus Christ, to bring salvation to the world. Into the town of Bethlehem, born in the lineage of David, comes our Lord Jesus Christ who is none other than the Savior of the world. Is it not amazing how two grieving, broken women with nothing to hang onto and nothing to look forward to, through commitment, love, and friendship blessed the world by giving us an outstanding psalmist and warrior king of Israel, David, and the Lord Jesus Christ, none other than the holy Son of God?

CONCLUSION

Rob Norris, at Four Presbyterian Church in Washington DC, tells the story of a young man in England who was engaged to a beautiful lady whom he loved deeply. But the young man was involved in a serious accident, which left him blind. In hospital, discovering that he had lost his sight, he sent for his fiancée. When she came to see him, she was very shaken and upset. After much thought and consideration, she told him that she wanted to break the engagement because she could not cope with his blindness. Dejected, hurt, and discouraged, the young man asked a nurse to write the following words on a pad, which became a well-known hymn of surrender to God's love:

> Oh, love that will not let me go.
> I rest my weary soul in Thee.
> I give thee back the life I owe,
> That in thine ocean depths its flow may richer, fuller be.[6]

Our inner peace need not depend on the fulfillment of a dream. Made in the image of God, we all have an in-built longing for God. As our dreams shatter, the mystery is that if we acknowledge the hurt, we find in the midst of the pathos, pain, and grief, the presence of the Eternal Love that will never let us go. And even though our dreams may shatter, like David, we can say, "When I awake, I will be satisfied with seeing your likeness" (Psalm 17:15).

REFERENCES

1. Langston Hughes, *In Perrine's Sound and Sense* ed. T. R. Arp and G. Johnson (Boston: Heinle & Heinle, 2002), 80.
2. Eckhart Tolle, *The Power of Now* (Nouato, California: New World Library, 2001), 23.
3. Alfred Tennyson, *In Memorium: 21* (1850).
4. Henri Nouwen, (personal communication when I served with him on the Faculty of Yale University Divinity School, 1977).
5. Quoted in *Ruth, the Romance of Redemption* by J. Vernon Mc Gee (Nashville, Tennessee: Thomas Nelson Publishers, 1943), 63.

6. George Matheson, *O Love That Will Not Let Me Go* (U.S.A., Lexicon Music Inc.), 135.

EPILOGUE: A LIFE OF
CONTEMPLATION OBSERVED

Since I left my island home at nineteen, many older people abroad have become close, warm friends. Sometimes an older friend, who can see linkages between the past, the present, and the future, offers a deeper quality of friendship. Henry was such a friend. A distinguished Connecticut businessman, he was also a very spiritual man, an elder in my church. I was around thirty years old and Henry was about seventy.

Henry seemed to know when I was struggling and going through a difficult time. I was running a research unit at Yale Medical School, and every two weeks or so Henry would call and invite me to lunch. We always ate at the same place, Chuck's Steakhouse (Henry came from Scottish stock and felt it offered the best value for money!). Henry would pick me up in his stately Cadillac, and we would drive together to Chuck's. Over lunch he would talk about his life, and I would share the issues in my life. He had a kind manner and was always very understanding. I saw him as a contemplative and holy person; he seemed to have a tolerance for failure and people who did not agree with him. Having a love for the young people in the church, he would make time to be involved in their lives and offer to help them as much as he could. He had particular interest in helping young men going into business. Henry and his wife Shirley were very close, and it was a beautiful sight on a Sunday morning to see them walk together into church. They were one, a wonderful married couple.

I returned to the Bahamas in 1980, but when I visited Yale on business three years later, I was keen to return the kindness that Henry had shown, so I invited him to Chuck's Steakhouse for lunch. When I picked up Henry that morning he was very quiet and seemed sad and worried. We didn't say much as we drove along to the eating-place. After we sat down Henry said, "David, I would like share something with you that is very painful but extremely important to my life. Sunday morning, about three weeks ago, Shirley woke up, looked at me in bed and asked who I was and what I was doing there. She claimed not to know me." After fifty years of marriage this was a dreadful shock. To cut a long story short, Shirley was diagnosed with Alzheimer's disease. Deteriorating quickly, she was placed in a special nursing home. Henry said the parting was extremely painful because for fifty years they had worked together, played together, and of course prayed together. After a very long silence, Henry reached over, looked me straight in the face, and said, "David, I have to make a very important decision. When Shirley became ill and had to go to the nursing home, I decided to move to Florida. As a healthy eighty-year-old, I felt there was a lot life in me yet. Being well off, I could enjoy the final years of my life not being bothered with the pain of a wife with Alzheimer's. But during my time of contemplative prayer a few mornings ago, I became convicted God wanted to teach me compassion before I died."

As Henry reviewed his life, he realized that although he had been a very successful businessman, he was a hard man who would not take slackness or nonsense from an employee. He had fired many young men because of a single failure or lateness. He said, "I was not compassionate or kind in business. I had a totally righteous outlook and as far as I was concerned, there was only one way: the right way. If you didn't do it my way, you could get out!" His conviction, through the spirit of God, was that before he went home to be with the Lord, God wanted to teach him compassion. Looking at me with tears in his eyes, he said, "I'm not going to go to Florida. This very morning I put my house on the market, and I am moving into the nursing home to care for Shirley. This is a very hard decision for me because I am such an independent person. I don't know how to care for a sick person or someone who rejects me. She pushes me away when I try to read to her or pray with her or feed her. But I feel strongly I should be with her."

A few weeks later I had the chance to speak with a social worker at the nursing home where Shirley and Henry were living. She said it was touching to see how lovingly Henry tried to feed Shirley. Sometimes Shirley would push his hand away, shouting, "Leave me alone!" Sometimes he would try to read the scripture to her and she would push the Bible out of his hands. But regardless of her resistance and obstinacy, Henry lovingly took care of her. About a year later I learned that Henry had died from a heart attack, leaving Shirley still living in the nursing home.

Thinking about this great man of God, I will never forget Henry saying that he felt the spirit of God showing him that although he had been very successful in business, active in the church, and committed to his spiritual journey, he lacked compassion. God convicted him, "You need to learn compassion. Your soul needs to grow in the air of compassion before you come home." The witness of the social worker indicated to me that my friend Henry was learning compassion in caring for his sick wife. And after learning the lesson of compassion, he was called home.

Contemplation is not some isolated sentimental experience; it is opening to the vision of God and then bowing in deep commitment to follow the mission of God's love in the world. Whether seen in the life of Mother Theresa of Calcutta or my friend Henry of Connecticut, contemplation of the love of God always expresses itself in compassion for those around us. Compassion is always the validation of true contemplation.